THE BRITISH AVANT-GARDE

THE BRITISH AVANT-GARDE
The Theory and Politics of Tradition

Josephine M. Guy

Lecturer in English

Leicester Polytechnic

HARVESTER
WHEATSHEAF

New York   London   Toronto   Sydney   Tokyo   Singapore

First published 1991 by
Harvester Wheatsheaf
66 Wood Lane End, Hemel Hempstead
Hertfordshire HP2 4RG
A division of
Simon & Schuster International Group

Typeset in 10/12 pt Plantin
by Pentacor PLC, High Wycombe, Bucks

Printed and bound in Great Britain by
Billing and Sons Ltd, Worcester

British Library Cataloguing in Publication Data

Guy, Josephine, *1963–*
    The British avant-garde : the theory and politics of
    tradition.
    1.   Avant garde arts. Political aspects, history
    I. Title
    700.9

    ISBN   0–7450–0776–7

1 2 3 4 5   95 94 93 92 91

Contents

Acknowledgements

Parts of the argument in the Introduction and in Chapter 1 have been rehearsed elsewhere, in an essay entitled 'The concept of tradition and late nineteenth-century British avant-garde movements' (*Prose Studies*, September, 1990), and in two essays written in collaboration with Ian Small: 'The French Revolution and the Avant-Garde' (in Ceri Crossley and Ian Small (eds.), *The French Revolution and British Culture*, Oxford: Oxford University Press, 1989, 141–55) and 'Usefulness in literary history' (*British Journal of Aesthetics*, Spring, 1991). The advice and encouragement of Dr Small throughout the writing of this book have been invaluable, and I should like to record my deep gratitude to him. Thanks are also due to Professor Bernard Bergonzi and Professor Kelsey Thornton for their useful comments on an early draft, and to Jackie Jones for her enthusiasm for the initial idea.

Introduction

F ew definitions have become so central to our understanding of the shape of literary and art history as that of avant-gardism. Yet the wide currency of the term is not matched by a comparable agreement about what it means. Rather the opposite: few definitions so assiduously theorised have remained so vexed and so elusive. In its popular usage, avant-gardism is generally taken to refer to a special kind of militant artistic or literary radicalism, believed to have originated some time in the middle or late nineteenth century. But among those theorists with a particular interest in avant-gardism, the exact nature of this radicalism is a much disputed issue. Also in dispute therefore is the 'canon' of artists and writers whose work can properly be said to embody 'authentic' avant-garde characteristics. Despite all this, in most instances where the term avant-garde is used it is assumed to be unproblematic; few critics and historians seem fully aware of the extent to which it is a contested concept. On closer examination, the term avant-garde assumes strangely chameleon-like qualities: its defining features vary widely according to the particular theorist who is describing it. So in one usage, 'the avant-garde' may refer to those artists and writers whose work is noteworthy for its formal or aesthetic innovation; in another, it may designate artists and writers who hold particular political views, and who self-consciously use their art in their service. In the former case avant-gardism defines aesthetic radicalism, and in the latter political radicalism. Histories based on these two definitions have naturally encompassed quite different groups of artists and writers.

1

One of the reasons why the concept of avant-gardism has been so protean is that the term has always been available for appropriation for specific, and usually very different, political or aesthetic ends. As I shall elaborate in Chapter 1, avant-gardism is an evaluative as well as a descriptive term, and the history of its use is also a history of competing aesthetic and political value judgements; most attempts to define avant-gardism have thus been prescriptive rather than simply descriptive. One of the aims of this book will be to uncover the hidden politics and unstated assumptions behind the various attempts to define avant-gardism; its larger ambition will be to contest the view, held by most specialists and non-specialists alike, that there is a single transhistorical phenomenon which can be defined as 'the avant-garde'. I shall argue that all attempts to define avant-gardism which begin with such a premiss are inadequate in that they do nothing more than replace one set of contested political or aesthetic value judgements with another. In order to reach a definition of avant-gardism which avoids evaluative criteria, and which can therefore genuinely claim to be comprehensive, it is necessary to view avant-garde politics in their cultural and historical specificity; the achievements of radical and innovative artists and writers must be measured in terms of their *own* culture and not ours – in terms, that is, of the specific intellectual, political, or aesthetic orthodoxies to which those artists and writers were opposing themselves. Properly speaking, then, the concept of a single and homogeneous avant-garde should be replaced by that of a complex plurality of avant-gardes. What all avant-garde movements will have in common is simply a self-conscious opposition to the past or tradition; where they will differ (as I shall demonstrate, sometimes quite radically) is in the particular forms which that opposition takes. The task of the historian is to discover *why* forms of avant-garde opposition differ – to discover, that is, the particular conditions which produce a particular form of avant-garde activity.

Underlying my suggestion that it is the specificity of avant-garde opposition which is important, there is a more general issue concerning the relationship between aesthetics and politics in art and literature. To attempt to define avant-gardism is merely to confront in a dramatic way a problem which is now endemic to literary and art historiography generally – the problem of the role of politics in those histories. Broadly speaking, it is possible to identify two sorts of literary and art history which correspond to the two kinds of definition of avant-gardism alluded to above. On the one hand, there are histories (such as those produced by formalists) which dwell upon the development of the stylistic or linguistic features within a particular genre. These kinds of histories would in their turn define avant-gardism in terms of formal or aesthetic innovation. On the other hand, there are 'political' histories, and these are now the dominant kind, virtually amounting to a new orthodoxy. They include Marxism, feminism and New Historicism, and they take as their primary subject the political and social preconditions for the production of texts and art works. Such histories would define as avant-garde those works of art and literature which have (or had) a subversive political function. As a rule these two kinds of histories coexist uneasily; but often, as with recent debates about feminism, that uneasy coexistence erupts into a deep antagonism. And this antagonism replicates, although on a grander scale, the disagreements over the nature of avant-gardism.

The major problem of this antagonism is that neither kind of history can agree on a common subject-matter or an appropriate methodology. The point is best illustrated by reference to literary histories problematise that givenness in that they see 'literariness' which has in recent years provided the most fertile ground for explicitly political theorists. In formal or 'aesthetic' literary histories, the concept of the 'literary' is taken as a given; but 'political' literary histories problematise that giveness in that they see 'literariness' simply as a construct of ideology. To put issues at their most general, the dispute is between an assumption that the aesthetic is autonomous (and thus a legitimate object of study), and the proposition that the whole concept of literature is politically determined – albeit covertly so – and that the historian's task is to uncover the ideological character of that determination. At the heart, then, of those problems usually referred to as 'the canon' is a disagreement about the nature of the relationship between aesthetics and politics. One view sees the aesthetic as separate, or at least separable, from political concerns, while the other sees it as being totally reducible to them. Indeed the distinctiveness of many recent 'political' histories lies in their claim to be a complete explanation of a work. Such histories dismiss as false the premisses of all other kinds of literary history on the grounds that those premisses in themselves are subject to prior political determinations. More precisely 'political' histories allege that judgements claimed to be aesthetic or literary ones disguise a set of political values. In this view, then, there can be no possible accommodation between 'aesthetic' and 'political' histories.

The questions which are begged by this opposition are two-fold. The first concerns the kind of relationship which could exist between an 'aesthetic' and a 'political' history. Are they, for instance, as radically opposed as some recent theorists have suggested? The second has to do with their relative utility. For many practising critics the two questions are aspects of a single issue, for literary and art histories need to be able to operate at a certain level of specificity in the sense that their most important use for the critic is the explanation of the individuality of texts and art works. Here, then, the ability of a 'political' history to accommodate an 'aesthetic' history in a large measure determines its usefulness. Nowhere is this general issue of the utility of literary and art history – of the ability of such histories to account for the specificity of literary and art works – more starkly set out than in the problems concerning contemporary definitions of avant-gardism.

In nearly all literary and art histories, and in all avant-garde theorising, discussion of the nature of the relationship between art and politics has been hampered by a restrictive definition of what the term 'political' refers to. Usually a work's political aspects are understood to be the ways it silently replicates an ideology; moreover that ideology is invariably understood to be a bourgeois one. Now at a local level this restrictive definition operates in most 'political' histories of avant-gardism. In these histories it is suggested that avant-garde art and literature function in a way which alerts the reader or viewer to the operations of ideology. Hence avant-gardism is characterised in terms of a radical, subversive – and so invariably left-wing or socialist – critique of bourgeois ideology. One problem with this view is immediately apparent. The case of a right-wing avant-garde, such as Italian Futurism, complicates generalisations about avant-garde politics, particularly those which reduce political dialogue to the narrow polarities of party politics. But there is also a second, more serious problem which is less obvious. It concerns the subordination of the aesthetic characteristics of art or literature to their political functions. In this view, the formal characteristics of, say, Realism are only of significance – and indeed of interest – in so far as they relate to a work's political functions. However, the complex history of Realism suggests that its devices have never been employed for a single or simple political end. This problem may be stated in general terms: it is impossible to draw up a taxonomy of formal or aesthetic features which precisely maps on to a category of political functions. In this respect, then, it is not surprising that 'political' definitions of avant-gardism, as I will demonstrate in Chapter 2, have been able to account for only a very few of the aesthetic or formal characteristics of avant-garde literary or art works.

The difficulty in explaining aesthetics wholly in terms of the political is not restricted to accounts of the politically subversive function of avant-garde works. Indeed it is a general problem of all 'political' histories which attempt to account for literary and art works solely in terms of their political determinants. It is quite clear that these histories are unable to account for the diversity of formal or aesthetic features in solely ideological terms without placing such a complex set of qualifications on the concept of ideology that it ceases to have any 'useful' explanatory power. The example of the diversity found in British modernism makes the point very clearly. T. S. Eliot's *The Waste Land* and Siegfried Sassoon's *Counter-Attack*, James Joyce's *Ulysses* and Arnold Bennett's *Riceyman's Steps* demonstrate a wide diversity of formal features, but they were all produced under the same broad set of social and political conditions, and the historian who wants to explain their diversity solely (or even principally) in terms of social determinants has to set about matching them precisely with a set of formal devices. Such a task is complicated by the coexistence of works whose political content is diverse, but whose formal devices are similar, and vice versa. A good example of such a problem is found in the work of British and Irish dramatists writing a little earlier. The plays of George Bernard Shaw, Oscar Wilde, and Henry Arthur Jones were produced under the same general ideological conditions and the same publishing and performance constraints, and they used broadly the same formal devices and resources of the 'well-made play'. But the political content of the plays is far from uniform. In order to explain such diversity in works produced at any historical moment, 'political' histories have to explain the selective nature of the determining processes which they allege are in operation; or they have to explain why the same ideological factors may produce such a diverse range of works. The problems which avant-garde historians have experienced in drawing up a taxonomy in which formal features map precisely on to a series or set of political functions are, then, only one instance of the more general problems in any attempt to explain the aesthetic solely in terms of the political. Moreover, if such histories cannot explain literary or art works in terms other than the political, then they will not be able to answer the most fundamental question – why politically motivated artists and writers chose such a medium in which to voice their radical views in the first instance; why, that is, they chose to be artists and writers at all. Paradoxically, then, to deny that art and literature – in this case avant-garde works – have a unique identity is to debar oneself from explaining the specificity of their political function. Indeed such a denial in turn obviates the need for the whole concept of avant-gardism, for the very term seeks to explain the *special* nature of artists' and writers' contribution to a political cause.

The paradox of recent 'political' explanations of avant-gardism is, then, as follows: if statements about social and political contexts are specific, then they have also to be narrowly based. However, if they are not narrow, such statements can only have force as generalisations. But generalisations, as I have indicated, say little about the nature of *individual* works, and are therefore of little practicable use to the historian. Thus to conduct a 'political' history which can distinguish between kinds of works and which is also adequate to explaining the diversity of formal features of those works it is necessary to pay attention to those influences which *cannot* be political or ideological. This suggestion does not, however, imply a simple (or naïve) return to 'aesthetic' or formal histories. Rather, it indicates a way in which those two kinds of history might be combined. In such a situation it might not be possible to identify a causal relationship between the formal qualities of a work and an ideology, except in the broadest terms – but such a restriction need not be taken to mean a 'depoliticised' history. Rather, the historian will only be able to isolate the specific circumstances in which formal choices might sometimes possess political significance, and hence the politics of formal devices may only be understood in relation to the specific circumstances as they are used.

It is precisely this way of understanding the relationship between aesthetics and politics – in terms, that is, of the ways in which formal choices *may* possess a political significance – which points to a more fruitful way of defining the radical politics of avant-gardism. It resolves the problem of matching formal devices to political functions, and it allows us to explain how literary and artistic avant-garde works function as literature and art.

PART I

Theory

CHAPTER 1

Preliminaries

Ever since the utopian socialist Henri de Saint-Simon applied the military metaphor to cultural matters over a hundred and fifty years ago, the concept of avant-gardism has been assiduously discussed by literary and art critics, cultural historians, sociologists and philosophers. However, as I have indicated, today the main legacy of this interest is a confusion, and at times profound disagreements, over what the term avant-gardism means and whom it designates. Rather than accept this situation, as at least one recent commentator has done,[1] I want to try to resolve current disagreements by finding some common ground between opposing views and then use it as a basis for re-theorising avant-gardism. But my interest in examining the concept of avant-gardism has also been motivated by another, more specific dissatisfaction. It is striking that in virtually all general histories of avant-gardism in Europe, radical and innovative British artists and writers of the late nineteenth century (and often of the twentieth century) are simply omitted; avant-gardism is generally assumed to be a Russian and continental flower with French, German and Italian hybrids but no British blooms.[2] In light of recent work on the radical sexual and textual politics of writers such as Oscar Wilde and Walter Pater, this omission now seems particularly unwarranted. Hence my main ambition in this book will be to use a new theory of avant-gardism to relocate the work of some late nineteenth-century British writers – principally Pater, Wilde and William Morris – within the main framework of avant-garde history.

In the first instance, however, it must be stressed that the concept of avant-gardism is not, and never has been, a neutral one. It does not just describe a movement; it also simultaneously evaluates it. The label avant-garde (often decided a posteriori) confers a particular status on the artist or writer to whom it is applied by designating his or her work as serious and important. Avant-garde iconoclasm and innovation are afforded respect, and sometimes admiration, precisely because they are assumed to be 'progressive' – the etymology of the term insists as much. More than just rebellious or attention seeking, work designated as avant-garde allegedly affects the future direction of art and literature in a positive way. However, the corollary of this is that iconoclastic and innovative work which is not labelled avant-garde is denied a similar status, and is thus not taken seriously. Designated idiosyncratic rather than prophetic, trivial rather than epoch-making, it is the work of the dilettante, poseur, or publicity seeker. When his or her work is labelled in this way, the writer or artist in question is relegated to a minor position in literary or art history and is judged to lack any serious engagement with major contemporary artistic and literary issues. It is precisely this kind of 'negative' labelling which goes a long way towards accounting for the marginal status endured by several late nineteenth-century writers – especially Wilde and Pater – up until the early 1970s.

It is clear that most theories and histories of avant-gardism, although they claim to be comprehensive, are in fact highly prescriptive. The 'avant-gardes' described by critics and theorists generally conform to some prior aesthetic or political criteria which are only rarely acknowledged. The debate between Theodor Adorno and Georg Lukács in the 1950s, for example, is only the most famous instance of the many disagreements over which particular artists and writers are to be viewed as avant-garde. The first task of a new theory of avant-gardism is therefore to make explicit these evaluative criteria, noting the main areas of confusion and disagreement which their existence has produced – the problems, for example, concerning different avant-garde canons and thus different histories of avant-gardism. The second task is to find a new way of defining avant-gardism which does not depend on evaluative criteria. This last task is not, however, as daunting as it at first sight may appear to be, for in fact there is one point upon which all avant-garde theorists and historians seem to agree (and therefore one which I take practically to be, as far as possible, value-free).

It is accepted as axiomatic that avant-garde movements define themselves in relation to the past – to tradition. Indeed, most historians go further and suggest that this has necessarily to take the form of an antagonistic relationship; thus, for example, Andreas Huyssen argues that 'the avant-garde' is the 'embodiment of anti-tradition', as it is the movement which 'fundamentally and on principle despised and denied all traditions'.[3] I want to take this basic assumption as my starting point for theorising avant-gardism; specifically, I want to examine what it means to talk of avant-gardism as being 'anti-tradition', for I shall suggest that this is, in fact, a highly problematic description. However, first it will be useful to clarify what is meant here by the term 'problematic' by referring to the current debate about the relationship between avant-gardism, post-modernism, and what is often referred to as the 'end', or 'death' of art.

One of the central issues in this debate is what many see to be the co-opting of avant-garde movements by the 'culture industry'. Avant-gardism, it is argued, has now become so successfully integrated into Western culture that it has itself become a tradition; but an avant-garde which has only itself to react against is a contradiction in terms. Hence, this argument goes, avant-gardism is now dead, and when we now talk of avant-gardism we are referring to a historical phenomenon; whatever post-modernism is, it therefore is not, and cannot be, the next avant-garde. It is not necessary to discuss here the consequences of this line of argument for the future of art and literature, nor to pursue the many refutations, particularly by Marxist critics, of its pessimism.[4] This view of the problem concerning the relationship between avant-garde movements and tradition, though important in itself, is in fact quite different from my concerns. In the first place, it assumes that such a relationship has only become problematic relatively recently and as a consequence of certain alleged changes in literary and artistic culture. Second, and more importantly, this argument holds the view that the relationship between avant-gardes and tradition is necessarily a wholly antagonistic one; such an assumption has not been challenged in this view in any significant way. In contrast, I want to argue that avant-garde movements have *always* had a problematic relationship with tradition, and that the nature of that relationship can only *sometimes* be understood in terms of a simple repudiation of tradition. (Indeed I would venture to suggest that a more thorough understanding of the dynamics of the relationship between avant-garde movements and tradition in the mid-nineteenth century, when avant-gardism is generally acknowledged to have begun, may go some way towards illuminating the problems concerning avant-gardism and post-modernism currently being debated.) Another, more specific example will serve to clarify my arguments further.

In an essay entitled 'The age of the avant-garde' which addresses some of the issues outlined above, Hilton Kramer identifies two different kinds of avant-garde. On the one hand, there are the revolutionaries who possess 'an intransigent radicalism that . . . cancels all debts to the past'; and on the other, the revisionists, 'champions of harmony and tradition . . . who are mindful, above all, of the continuity of culture'.[5] In the first group Kramer places Dada and Surrealism, and in the second, Matisse, Picasso, Eliot, Yeats, Schoenberg and Stravinsky. Having noted these two quite different attitudes towards tradition within avant-gardism, Kramer argues that:

> given the dynamics of modernism, where only consequences count, *this difference proves to be nugatory.* For Picasso prepares the way for Duchamp, and Duchamp's art has nowhere to go except the museum, where its presence does indeed modify the 'existing moments' in a way Eliot had not foreseen. It deprives them – and us – of their essential seriousness. Duchamp's legendary assault on the work of art as traditionally conceived . . . has the effect of consigning the idea of tradition and the museum itself to a limbo of arbitrary choices and gratuitous assertions. Which is exactly what our culture has become.[6]

Kramer's argument raises several issues worth pursuing. The first relates to his typology of avant-gardism which aligns Stravinsky and Schoenberg and sets them against Dadaism and Surrealism. In fact, as Theodor Adorno noted, there are at least as many differences between Stravinsky's and Schoenberg's respective attitudes towards tradition as there are between either of them and Dadaism and Surrealism. Moreover, Schoenberg himself exhibited different attitudes towards tradition at different stages in his career. Kramer's typology, in other words, obscures at least as many differences as it actually illuminates. The second issue concerns the kind of history which Kramer is tracing. It is an odd kind of historiography which bases an evaluation of the achievements of avant-garde artists principally upon their consequences for the present – which chastises Eliot, that is, for failing to anticipate Duchamp's 'readymades'. In fact this tendency to make a posteriori judgements, to castigate avant-garde artists and writers for not answering, or for failing to predict, problems which they could not possibly have foreseen is common among avant-garde theorists and historians. Similar conclusions are reached by Kramer's opponents on the left who use exactly the same methodological strategy – namely, the reading on to avant-garde movements a certain set of political ambitions, often defined in terms of contemporary concerns, which are then judged not to have been achieved. Richard Rorty has presented a convincing critique of this kind of 'false' historiography which he refers to as 'doxography', and in keeping with his general criticisms, there are particularly good reasons for rejecting the evaluative function of such avant-garde labelling.[7] Finally, the third, and most important issue which Kramer's argument raises, and the one which he is conspicuous in ignoring, is the question of *why* avant-garde artists and writers adopt different attitudes towards tradition. Only by answering this very basic question is it possible to appreciate, and subsequently evaluate, the effectiveness of avant-garde polemic. In contrast to Kramer, then, I am suggesting that the differences in attitudes towards tradition which are exhibited by various avant-garde artists and writers are fundamental; indeed they are central to understanding what is meant by avant-gardism.

The defining thesis of a new theory of avant-gardism will be the relationship between avant-garde movements and tradition, and the main objective of such a theory is to describe the conditions which determine the nature of this relationship. It is my argument that these conditions are fundamentally *intellectual* rather than social or political, for the manner in which avant-garde artists and writers define themselves in relation to tradition is determined, in the first instance, by the general attitudes towards the past within their particular culture. This is not to suggest that avant-garde movements necessarily partake of these general attitudes, but only that they define themselves in relation to them. The degree to which it is conceivable, or appropriate, for them to be anti-tradition is therefore severely circumscribed by whatever view of the past is dominant within their particular culture. So, for example, in France, where the French Revolution produced new ways of thinking about the past, and where the idea of historical rupture virtually became an orthodoxy in the nineteenth century, repudiation of tradition is very common among French avant-garde artists and writers. In other words, if avant-gardism is defined as necessarily anti-tradition, then it is clear that the intellectual conditions in France were ideal for the development of avant-gardism. The relationship between avant-gardism and tradition is unproblematic in France. But in Britain, where in the nineteenth century the dominant view of the past was Whiggish gradualism, and where the concept of constitutional continuity was central, the definition of avant-gardism as necessarily anti-tradition becomes problematic. British artists and writers, circumscribed by British orthodoxies about the past, clearly did not have the same intellectual freedom as their French contemporaries to repudiate tradition: such a strategy was simply inappropriate to the British intellectual climate. Hence it is the case that even the most innovative of British writers and artists were correspondingly very much concerned to place themselves *within* rather than *against* a tradition.

The problem then becomes one of how to place these British artists and writers and how to evaluate their work. In view of the differences between them and their French contemporaries, how, for example, can they also be considered avant-garde? Histories of avant-gardism have typically solved this problem by the simple expedient of denying them avant-garde status, arguing that writers such as Pater or Wilde are 'conventional' or not really 'revolutionary'. This has been the case because the French model of an avant-garde politics of tradition has usually been assumed to be the only appropriate one; to be an artistic revolutionary anywhere and at any time, so the argument goes, necessarily entails simple repudiation of tradition.[8] Now in contrast, I want to argue that this kind of generalisation about the politics of avant-gardism is quite unfounded because clearly there can be more than one way of politically subverting a tradition. Rather than repudiate it altogether, it is possible to challenge the concept of tradition equally subversively by 'using' it, as British artists and writers did, to authorise non-conventional practices. In other words, if the attitudes towards tradition exhibited by British avant-gardes are seen as a response to the peculiarities of the British intellectual climate, then they represent an entirely appropriate political strategy; they are just as 'oppositional' in their *own* context as those of their French contemporaries.[9] To put this argument in more general terms: we may only understand the politics of a particular avant-garde after we understand the attitude which that avant-garde adopts towards tradition; and that attitude may only be understood in terms of contemporary cultural orthodoxies about the past. An intellectual context is thus the basic reference point by which avant-garde politics have meaning.

This way of defining the concept of avant-gardism has several important implications for avant-garde theorising. It suggests that since orthodoxies about the past differ from one culture to the next, it is clearly not possible to posit, a priori, a set of political strategies which will be common to all avant-gardes in all countries and at all times. It is not possible to outline a set of strategies common to all avant-gardes within one country since over time attitudes towards the past in that country may change. Avant-garde politics, in other words, are historically and culturally specific. This in turn suggests that a comprehensive theory of avant-gardism cannot, therefore, be a 'political' theory. A theory which seeks to define avant-gardism principally in terms of a specific political function has to be inadequate since it is clearly not possible to make valid generalisations about the politics of all avant-gardes. Indeed, as I have indicated, those theories of avant-gardism which have tried to generate a political explanation of it, have been conspicuous in their failure to account for a significant number of radical and innovative artists and writers – especially British ones. However, if a theory of avant-gardism cannot be political in this way, it can still define avant-gardism intellectually and may thus still talk about politics. The principal difference between the two approaches lies in the kinds of explanation which each offers. An intellectual theory of avant-gardism is concerned with establishing the *conditions* which make avant-garde politics possible in the first instance; but a political theory of avant-gardism is concerned with describing the *consequences* or *success* of some predetermined prescriptions for appropriate political action. An intellectual theory of avant-gardism will thus pose a quite different set of questions from other theories; and these in turn will have some important implications for avant-garde historiography. If, as I have suggested, an examination of the intellectual conditions for avant-garde politics reveals substantial differences between the polemic of the individual avant-garde movements, then it can no longer be possible to talk about *the* avant-garde as if it were a transcultural, transhistorical phenomenon; such a phenomenon clearly does not exist. Neither is it possible to have a single history of 'the avant-garde'. The only history of avant-gardism which may be allowed is the combined histories of the several, quite separate avant-garde movements which are culturally and temporally specific.

How then would an 'intellectual' theory of avant-gardism work? In the first place, it will have to be based on premisses similar to those of intellectual history; it would assume, that is, that literary and artistic practices do not exist isolated from other forms of intellectual activity, but rather that they can only be fully understood within the general ideational context of the society of which they are a part. Therefore, establishing the intellectual conditions which make a particular literary or artistic practice possible will involve examining other, apparently unrelated disciplines of knowledge in order to describe a sociology of knowledge, for what happens in other disciplines may – in the senses I have described – have an important bearing on what artists and writers 'do'. For example, where the conditions for avant-garde activity are determined by general attitudes within a culture towards the past, it will be necessary to look primarily at historiography and sociology, because these disciplines necessarily have most influence in shaping attitudes towards the past within any culture. It may also be necessary to look at other, less obviously relevant disciplines because explanatory concepts developed in one discipline are closely related to the explanations and concepts in other contemporary disciplines. Not only do disciplines 'borrow' concepts from each other – sociology, for example, in the nineteenth century drew freely upon some of the assumptions of historiography – but they are also sometimes in competition with each other to explain the same phenomena. In other words, it will also be necessary to consider the intellectual *authority* of the particular discipline in question in order to establish the general currency of its explanations in a particular culture at a particular point in time. Thus, to take the same example: in order to determine the intellectual conditions for avant-garde activity, it will be necessary to look first at the attitudes towards the past which are developed by historiography and sociology, and then to examine the social and intellectual authority of those two disciplines in order to determine whether or not those attitudes were widely accepted. Only then will it be possible to determine the degree to which the concepts and explanatory models developed by these two disciplines prevented or allowed avant-garde activity.

The most significant difference between this use of contextual information and that usually employed by cultural historians and literary and art critics is that it views an ideational context as an integrated whole. In order to see that ideational whole, it is necessary to establish a plausible connection between concepts developed in any particular discipline and their possible use in specific literary and artistic practices, and then to establish also the mechanisms for such a use. The key to understanding these mechanisms, as I have suggested, lies in the prestige and hence the authority enjoyed by any particular discipline at any one time. Moreover, this authority is always relative – it cannot be comprehended in isolation from other neighbouring disciplines. So this particular notion of intellectual history views literary and artistic practices as being an integral part of a complex network of ideas and concepts, central to which is the idea of intellectual authority.[10] The principal advantage of this approach to 'contextualisation' lies in the precision, or specificity, of the relationships it describes. Many attempts to connect works of art and literature with their culture (intellectual or political) draw attention only to the contiguity of events or ideas. Rarely is there any explanation of how precisely ideas from one domain or discipline connect, or influence, practices in another. In this respect it is worth noting in passing that recent attempts by certain 'new-historicist' critics to persuade us of the relevance of what seem to be increasingly obscure or marginal texts, has coincided with a tendency to describe the relationship between those texts and the work in question purely metaphorically. Stephen Greenblatt's essays on the relationship between certain works by Shakespeare and what he terms 'social energies' is one of the most striking examples of this practice of offering as explanation what is in fact an observation of mere coincidence or contiguity.[11]

However, despite – or perhaps because of – its claim to specificity, an 'intellectual' theory, as I have outlined it, still has some important limitations. It must be stressed that the relationships which it can describe between an ideational context and specific literary and artistic practices, such as avant-gardism, are not *causal* ones. Thus, for example, in a culture where there is a concept of historical rupture there will not always be an avant-garde which is anti-tradition – there may not be any avant-garde in that culture at all. However, where there is an avant-garde which is anti-tradition, then it will have necessarily been made possible by a concept of historical rupture. In other words, the availability of certain concepts can only be established as *necessary* but not sufficient conditions for the existence of certain literary and artistic practices.[12] In this sense then the theory proposed here is not a complete theory of avant-gardism; it cannot, for example, claim the kind of comprehensiveness of Renato Poggioli's *The Theory of the Avant-Garde* which purported to be a definitive account of the sociological and psychological causes of all avant-garde movements.[13] However, the theory proposed here can claim a different kind of comprehensiveness, for it provides a method by which all avant-garde movements may potentially be understood and evaluated within one frame of reference. Indeed, it may even be able to explain why post-modernism, which Poggioli's theory conspicuously fails to account for, may simply be another species of avant-garde.

·My discussion of avant-gardism in the following chapters will be divided into two sections. The first will examine theoretical issues. In Chapter 2 I shall outline the ambiguities, disagreements and omissions – particularly those concerning nineteenth-century British avant-gardes – which have been the result of the current multiplicity of avant-garde theories and histories. The discussion in this chapter will refer particularly to the two major theories of avant-gardism to have been produced recently – by Renato Poggioli and Peter Bürger – since they can be seen as representing two different and mutually exclusive traditions of avant-garde theorising. In their turn, they have been largely responsible both for the general confusion about what the concept of avant-gardism means and, more specifically, for the marginalisation of late nineteenth-century British avant-garde movements. I will also outline in this chapter a new 'intellectual' theory of avant-gardism along the lines discussed above, one which is capable of resolving the problems inherent in Poggioli's and Bürger's theories. In Chapter 3 I shall use this new theory to describe the conditions for avant-garde activity in late nineteenth-century Britain, and to contrast them with those which obtained in France. Chapter 4 will then discuss, in general terms, the beginnings of the emergence of avant-gardism in Britain in the mid-1870s. It will concentrate on two issues: the politics of tradition – specifically, the manner in which the 'use' of tradition within Aestheticism involved radically subverting established views on how a tradition should function; and the politics of language in the complex debates in the 1880s about the function of obscurity. Chapters 5, 6 and 7 will apply these insights to the work of three British writers – Walter

Pater, William Morris and Oscar Wilde respectively. The aim here will be to describe the different ways in which each of these writers approached the issue, rendered problematic by the British intellectual climate, of the relationship between the radical or innovative artist and tradition.

Notes

1. See Diana Crane, *The Transformation of the Avant-Garde* (Chicago: University of Chicago Press, 1987). Although Crane notes that there are many current, and often contradictory, definitions of avant-gardism, she makes no attempt to resolve these differences.
2. See, for example, Theda Shapiro, *Painters and Politics: The European avant-garde and society, 1900–1925* (Amsterdam: Elsevier, 1976).
3. Andreas Huyssen, 'The Search for Tradition: Avant-garde and post modernism in the 1970s', *New German Critique*, 22 (Winter, 1981), 24 and 33.
4. See, for example, the *Partisan Review*, 39, 3 (1972) which is largely devoted to discussing the implications of this line of argument. After an essay by Richard Gilman entitled 'The idea of the avant-garde', various critics, poets and historians (including Allen Ginsberg, Clement Greenberg, Harold Rosenberg, Tony Tanner and Christopher Lasch) contribute brief comments on the 'new cultural conservatism'. See also articles by Jürgen Habermas, Peter Bürger, Anthony Giddens and Andreas Huyssen in the edition of the *New German Critique* (ibid.) devoted to post-modernism; and the essay by Ferenc Fehér, 'What is beyond art? On theories of post modernity' in Ferenc Fehér and Agnes Heller (eds.), *Reconstructing Aesthetics* (Oxford: Basil Blackwell, 1986), 60–76.
5. Hilton Kramer, 'The age of the avant-garde' in *The Age of the Avant-Garde* (London: Secker and Warburg, 1974), 7.
6. Ibid. 18. (The emphasis is mine.)
7. Richard Rorty, 'The historiography of philosophy: four genres' in Richard Rorty, J. B. Schneewind and Quentin Skinner (eds.), *Philosophy in History: Essays on the historiography of philosophy* (Cambridge: Cambridge University Press, 1984).
8. In allowing for different attitudes towards tradition Kramer is, of course, an exception here.
9. Though Kramer saw the two attitudes towards tradition which he identified as leading eventually to the same dead end, he nevertheless viewed the 'revisionists' as initially less destructive, or subversive than the revolutionaries. I differ from him, therefore, in suggesting that in their own contexts each strategy was equally subversive.
10. Recently Ian Small has used a similar approach to uncover the conditions for critical writing in the nineteenth century, and together

we have used this methodology to throw some light on the present crisis in English. See Ian Small, *Conditions for Criticism: Authority, knowledge and literature in the late nineteenth century* (Oxford: Clarendon Press, 1991); Ian Small and Josephine Guy, 'Critical opinion: English in crisis', *Essays in Criticism*, 39 (July 1989), 185–95; and 'English in crisis – II', *Essays in Criticism*, 40 (July 1990) 185–97; and Josephine Guy, Ian Small and Marcus Walsh, 'The profession of English', *English Association Newsletter*, nos 131 and 132.

11. Stephen Greenblatt, *Shakespearian Negotiations* (Oxford: Clarendon Press, 1988).

12. In respect of this distinction it is worth noting the claim made by Linda Dowling in her recent attempt to explain Decadence in terms of contemporary debates within philology. In arguing that Decadence was fundamentally a linguistic phenomenon produced by the tension between a Romantic philology and that of the neo-grammarians, Bopp and Grimm, recently imported from Germany, Dowling claims to have described a causal relationship. However, because she looks at philology in isolation from other kinds of intellectual activity, she cannot describe the authority of its concepts and explanatory models; Dowling is unable, that is, to establish the currency of philology's explanations and therefore also unable to demonstrate conclusively the influence of this rather esoteric body of knowledge on specific literary and artistic practices. Her argument as it stands can therefore only be at the level of a somewhat unlikely hypothesis. See Linda Dowling, *Language and Decadence in Victorian Fin-de-Siècle* (Princeton: Princeton University Press, 1986).

13. Renato Poggioli, *The Theory of the Avant-Garde* (Cambridge, Mass.: Harvard University Press, 1968).

CHAPTER 2

Some problems with defining avant-gardism

The nature of avant-gardism has been debated for over a hundred and fifty years, but it is only relatively recently, in the past two or three decades, that it has been the subject of any rigorous theoretical enquiry. The first example of this kind of attention was Renato Poggioli's seminal work of the early 1960s, *The Theory of the Avant-Garde*. His was the first attempt since José Ortega y Gasset's brief defence of the 'new' art in the 1920s to offer a comprehensive theory which could account for all kinds of cultural avant-gardism. Of course there had been earlier theorists with an interest in avant-garde movements – notably the famous group of Marxist critics and artists in Germany – Georg Lukács, Theodor Adorno and Walter Benjamin – who, during the 1930s and 1950s, engaged in a series of debates which addressed the nature and function of avant-garde art. However, these critics were not concerned with explaining the origins and causes of cultural avant-gardism in the systematic manner attempted by Poggioli; their interest in avant-garde movements was, in a sense, tangential to other, larger political concerns. However, Marxism's interest in avant-gardism has been revived more recently in a theory designed to challenge the hegemony enjoyed by Poggioli since the 1960s. Peter Bürger's *Theory of the Avant-Garde* (first published in German in 1974) was a self-conscious engagement both with Poggioli's work and with fellow Marxists such as Adorno and Lukács; indeed it is the only study since Poggioli's *Theory* to claim the same kind of comprehensiveness. However, despite the pre-eminence of these two critics, their work in fact stands at the head of two long established, but quite separate traditions of thinking about avant-gardism.

The first of these traditions comprises those critics who emphasise the 'political' aspects of avant-gardism; who see avant-garde artists and writers using art principally in the service of ideological concerns, their aim being to bring about wider changes in the nature of society. The second tradition comprises those who stress the pre-eminence of the 'aesthetic'. In this view the main concern of avant-garde artists and writers is seen to be the disruption or replacement of accepted formal devices; to use Victor Shklovsky's term, avant-garde art defamiliarises conventional literary language, artistic symbols and iconography. Moreover, these two different ways of thinking about avant-gardism have in practice become translated into mutually exclusive definitions: avant-garde artists and writers can be either politically radical or artistically radical, but they can rarely be both. Broadly speaking, Bürger, along with most other Marxist critics, belongs to the first tradition in that his primary concern is with the political function of avant-garde art and literature. Poggioli, on the other hand, belongs to the second tradition since his exclusive emphasis on formal innovation and on the 'alienated' state of avant-garde artists and writers explicitly precludes them from having any specific social or political functions. The existence of these two opposing views of avant-gardism has led to confusion and disagreement over what avant-gardism means, and, more importantly, whom the term 'avant-garde' designates.

In fact there are two areas in which this problem of definition is felt. The less acute concerns those artists and writers who seem to fit one definition but not the other. For example, an emphasis on the political constructs a canon in which artists and writers such as Gustave Courbet and William Morris, both of whom were concerned principally with political rather than aesthetic questions, are given priority; in this definition writers such as Théophile Gautier and Gerard Manley Hopkins, who aimed at formal experimentation and for whom aesthetic innovation was of paramount importance, are either excluded altogether or marginalised. Emphasis on the latter category – that is, on the aesthetic – simply reverses these exclusions and constructs another quite different canon. However, a more acute and separate problem concerns those artists and writers, principally British ones, who cannot easily be accommodated by either tradition, and who have thus remained absent from most avant-garde histories. Some examples of this 'ambiguity' and 'exclusion' will illustrate the unfortunate consequences of these mutually opposing definitions.

One artist whose avant-garde status has recently been the subject of debate is the French painter Gustave Courbet. The first major study of Courbet to discuss his work in terms of its claim to avant-garde status was Linda Nochlin's *Gustave Courbet: A study of style and society*.[1] Nochlin's main ambition was to show Courbet as a revolutionary, drawing attention to the relationship between the iconoclasm of his early realist works and the ideals of the 1848 Revolution. In her final assessment of Courbet, however, she comes to a rather unexpected conclusion: 'despite the undeniably innovating quality of Courbet's achievement,' she argues, 'if one were forced to draw the boundary line between the past and the present in the art of the nineteenth century, one would inevitably draw it in 1863 with Manet's *Olympia* or his *Déjeuner sur l'herbe* rather than in 1850 with Courbet's *Burial at Ornans*.'[2] The reason for this decision is made clear in a later essay:

> If we take 'avant-garde' out of its quotation marks, we must come to the conclusion that what is generally implied by the term begins with Manet rather than Courbet. For implicit – and perhaps even central – to our understanding of avant-gardism is the concept of alienation – psychic, social, ontological – utterly foreign to Courbet's approach to art and to life.[3]

The 'understanding' which Nochlin refers to is one based largely on Renato Poggioli's definition of avant-gardism. Indeed at the time when Nochlin was writing Poggioli's work was influential in America. His view of avant-gardim, as Nochlin testifies, was taking on the dimensions of an orthodoxy. So, despite all the compelling evidence which she adduces to the contrary, Nochlin finally accedes to Poggioli's judgement and denies Courbet 'authentic' avant-garde status. However, her decision seems unsatisfactory, not least because earlier in the same essay she cites, as an equally authoritative source, the work of Donald Drew Egbert.[4] Now Egbert, in contrast to Poggioli, traced a history of avant-gardism which gave priority to politicised art. This history valorised those avant-garde artists who, following Henri de Saint-Simon's original injunctions, attempted to produce an art in which stylistic and formal elements were subservient to the artist's larger social responsibilities. Here again a representative artist was Gustave Courbet: his overtly social and political concerns made him, in Egbert's eyes, the perfect type of avant-garde artist. The problem then with Nochlin's account of

Courbet is that she seems to be using at one and the same time two quite different and competing definitions of avant-gardism. Her final accession to Poggioli's views appears arbitrary, even perverse, because on the face of it, it is so uncritical.[5]

However, Nochlin's judgements on Courbet have not met with universal acceptance; more recently the problem of Courbet's avant-garde status resurfaced in the objections raised by Charles Rosen and Henri Zerner to the Realist Exhibition mounted by Gabriel Weisberg for the Cleveland Museum of Art in 1980.[6] Rosen and Zerner accused Weisberg of a revisionism, symptomatic, they claimed, of much contemporary American art-history, which tended to deny both the centrality and efficacy of avant-garde movements in art-history. More specifically, Rosen and Zerner took issue with the relative insignificance assigned to an artist such as Courbet in so comprehensive an exhibition. Such a relegation, they argued, had the effect of erasing the radical qualities which patently distinguished Courbet from contemporaries such as Bonvin. The exhibition's fundamental mistake, they alleged, was to confuse Realism, an avant-garde movement, with the Realistic, a style of representation which favoured verisimilitude. Rosen and Zerner tried to reassert Courbet's claims to avant-garde status, and their means of doing so are instructive. Caught in the same dilemma as Nochlin – namely, the problem of how to assimilate legitimately into an avant-garde tradition an artist as clearly political in his concerns as Courbet without a complete denial of the politics of his work – they tried to find a solution by defining Courbet's work in terms of *stylistic* rather than political radicalism. For them Courbet's closest literary relation was Flaubert: both figures were more concerned with the means of representation rather than with what was being represented. In Rosen and Zerner's argument, Courbet's goal – 'the destruction . . . of the old idealizing rhetorical tradition' – was comparable to Flaubert's conception of *Madame Bovary* as 'a book about nothing': both are part of the same avant-garde impetus towards the 'disappearance of the subject' where 'subject' is defined as 'that which prolongs the thoughts of the spectator beyond the representation: the narrative significance, the moral, the meaning'.[7] Rosen and Zerner thus appropriate but invert the argument employed by Nochlin to deny avant-garde status to Courbet: what characterises his art in their view is now not political but stylistic radicalism. The point here is that once again the conceptual framework used by

Poggioli to define avant-gardism has not been challenged in any significant way, and this despite the fact that early in the essay Rosen and Zerner make a plea for a more flexible, or 'mobile' definition of avant-gardism. All they have in fact succeeded in doing is to relocate the grounds of Courbet's radicalism from one category to another. The ambiguity over Courbet's avant-garde status is thus not really resolved. Courbet simply slips from one category to the other, and those categories themselves, with their protean and accommodating qualities, are never properly challenged.

However, the problems concerning the avant-garde status of certain other artists and writers cannot be solved even by this process of reversal. Courbet, though with some distortion, can be made to 'fit' at least one definition of avant-gardism – but the majority of late nineteenth-century oppositional British artists and writers fit neither definition very easily with the result that they have generally been omitted altogether from most histories and theories of avant-gardism. In this respect one prominent example, Oscar Wilde, will serve for the rest.

The few notable attempts to include Wilde in avant-garde history (without fundamentally challenging the existing categories of definition), are informative only in so far as they illustrate the difficulty of the task. Most critics interested in Wilde as a potential avant-garde figure have focused attention upon his *political* radicalism – on the espousal of anarchist doctrines in some of his works.[8] In practice, however, finding conclusive evidence for Wilde as a political radical, in this narrow sense of the term, is fraught with problems, the most debilitating of which is that there are only two possible texts which lend themselves to such a reading, *Vera, or The Nihilists* (which is Wilde's only 'political' play and which was not performed publically in his lifetime) and 'The Soul of Man Under Socialism'. Such a limited (and slight) selection from the *oeuvre* is clearly an insufficient ground upon which to establish Wilde's avant-garde credentials. Moreover, even if this strategy is abandoned in place of examining the content of Wilde's work for evidence of his promotion of radical *sexual* politics, the problem is still not resolved; such a function can only be ascribed to the *oeuvre* by means of an equally partial reading of his work.[9] The paradox presented by Wilde's iconoclasm is that evidence for the promotion of radical political doctrines in his writing is only rarely to be found: Wilde cannot convincingly be accommodated to a tradition of political radicalism, but nor can he be accommodated to a tradition of aesthetic radicalism. Wilde's work is marked by the frequency of its borrowings – or, to use a term favoured by many critics, its plagiarism – and by its use of traditional forms; the society dramas, for example, draw upon French 'well-made plays' and Victorian melodrama. In fact Wilde's iconoclasm lies in the manner in which he subverted traditional forms by using them in contexts which undermined their conventional significance.[10] But existing accounts of aesthetic and political radicalism have no way of accounting for such strategies. Ironically, given the existing definitions of avant-gardism, it is a minor work such as Robert Tressell's *The Ragged Trousered Philanthropists* which has a greater claim to avant-garde status in Britain, because that book, while traditional in form, is subversive in its political content. Naturally, however, a British avant-garde composed of writers such as Tressell will seem unimportant.

The principal reason for these problems of definition, felt most acutely in the case of British oppositional writers and artists, is that the two different ways of thinking about avant-gardism both assume that they are describing a single kind of phenomenon; hence the tendency to use the term 'the avant-garde'. There is little or no attempt in either tradition to discriminate between the polemic of avant-garde movements in each category – it is assumed that all political radicals are substantially the same, and so too are all aesthetic radicals. In other words the isolation and separation of the 'political' and the 'aesthetic' has imposed the only grounds for differentiating between avant-garde movements.[11] This rather crude method of discrimination, however, begs many more questions than it answers, and the most important, if only because they reveal the inadequacy of these definitions so startlingly, are those concerning the dating of cultural avant-gardism.[12]

Generally speaking, the tradition which emphasises the political radicalism of avant-gardism traces its origins to the writing of Henri de Saint-Simon and the tradition of social thought which his work brought about.[13] In that tradition, art and the artist are seen as having primarily a social function. Although Saint-Simon quite naturally distinguished between the specific tasks of artists, scientists and social administrators, he saw their final functions – the creation of the new post-Revolutionary state – possessing large areas of similarity: artists had a special social role, and hence particular obligations towards the state. Most accounts of socialist realism trace its ancestry back to statements such as these. Importantly, then, in this view avant-gardism begins in 1850, with an artist such as Gustave Courbet because, it is argued, he was one of the first artists to produce an art in which stylistic and formal elements are placed in the service of an artist's larger social responsibilities. The second tradition – which emphasises aesthetic innovation – also locates the origins of avant-gardism in the writing of Saint-Simon.[14] However, this second tradition does not date the first authentic avant-garde movement until the mid-1860s with the more mature work of Manet because the emphasis on stylistic innovation limits the designation of avant-gardism to those later artists and writers who transferred the radical Revolutionary critique of social forms into the domain of stylistic (or aesthetic) forms – artists, that is, who were concerned to adapt or replace aspects of traditional symbols and icons to produce an appropriate contemporary iconography or symbolism. The problem here is that if the basic historical distinction is between two kinds of artistic avant-garde, the political and the stylistic or aesthetic, then the relationship between them becomes a vexed one. Why, for example, did one give way to the other? Historical accounts of the formation of avant-garde movements rarely seem aware of this question. Even the most sophisticated proponent of this history, Donald Drew Egbert, suggests only a mechanism, and not a reason for this change. He argues that the aesthetic avant-garde came about because of artists' growing alienation from the 'state as represented by official academies of art under monarchic or bourgeois control'.[15] However, this account of the mechanism for the change, whatever its logical merits, is factually incorrect. For the two kinds of avant-garde – the 'political' and the 'stylistic' – were contemporaneous and not consecutive: in France Courbet and Gautier were contemporaries; in Britain so were Morris and Wilde. Such shortcomings lead inevitably to suspicions about the fundamental historiography behind observations such as Egbert's. However, if Egbert is incorrect, then the opposite question is pertinent: why did (and how could) these two traditions exist side by side?

These two problems – of 'definition' and 'dating' – produced by the existing ways of thinking about avant-gardism, strongly suggest the need for a new, and more subtle method for discriminating between the different forms of avant-garde polemic, since differences between avant-gardes clearly cannot be accounted for solely in terms of aesthetic or political radicalism. It is not simply that these two categories fail to further our understanding of *why* avant-gardes are different; more importantly, they severely distort the *nature* of those differences. As the brief example of Wilde suggests, and later chapters will demonstrate, the aesthetic and the political are not mutually exclusive categories. What is needed, then, is a much more sophisticated account of the relationship between aesthetics and politics. Before addressing this issue, it is useful to look in more detail at the ways in which the two paradigmatic theories of avant-gardism by Poggioli and Bürger have tried to explain that relationship. The ways in which each has approached this issue suggest, in a negative sense, some of the pitfalls which lie in wait for avant-garde theorising. Moreover, the works of Bürger and Poggioli have the added advantage of demonstrating very clearly the limitations of such theories in accounting for late nineteenth-century British oppositional writers and artists. Indeed it is the 'case' of what I shall provisionally term 'British avant-gardism' which most seriously exposes the limitations of both their theories.

Poggioli had two ambitions in *The Theory of the Avant-Garde*: to describe and categorise the many features of avant-gardism, and to give an account of the sociological and political conditions which make it possible. Thus he selected two features of avant-gardism (non-conformity and alienation) as being 'dominant'; and the rest (anti-traditionalism, experimentalism, obscurity and the search for novelty) were organised under four 'aspects' which he called activism, antagonism, nihilism and agonism. In Poggioli's view the necessary condition for avant-gardism was a background of political liberty – typically a Western democracy – because the avant-garde could only exist in a climate where 'otherness' was acknowledged as a possibility, if only on a conceptual level. It was this interdependence which characterised the contradictory or 'dialectical' relationship between avant-garde movements and the bourgeois society they so relentlessly attacked. For Poggioli, the audience for this reactionary art was always an intellectual élite whose appreciation of stylistic innovation was based on a willingness to embrace the 'new' sympathetically.

In a perceptive review of Poggioli's *Theory*, Peter Jones highlights two problems related to Poggioli's definition of avant-gardism in terms of certain necessary features. The first problem is the circularity of the thesis. Jones asks, 'what would, or could, falsify Poggioli's thesis? What counter-examples could be produced that would fail to fit the account? There is more than a whiff of suspicion that Poggioli does not admit counter-examples; candidates are either made to fit or are disqualified as art.'[16] This suspicion is justified by the virtual omission from Poggioli's account of late nineteenth-century British oppositional writers and artists, presumably on the grounds that at least two of his defining features – alienation and anti-traditionalism – are absent from the work of figures such as Algernon Swinburne, Walter Pater and Oscar Wilde. (The reason for Morris's exclusion – his interest in using art for explicitly political ends – has been alluded to above.) However, a number of British literary and cultural historians have used terms which are completely compatible with Poggioli's account of European avant-gardism to describe the antagonistic relationship which Swinburne, Pater and Wilde had with their culture.[17] When the work (and indeed the personal lives) of these writers are viewed in the context of specific debates about the social and moral function of art and literature in late nineteenth-century Britain, then the opposition of their writing to bourgeois culture is easy to see. Briefly, the work of Swinburne, Pater and Wilde engaged with one of the most contentious political issues of the day, famously addressed by Matthew Arnold in *Culture and Anarchy*. In order to perform the educative and 'civilising' functions which Arnold wanted to attribute to it, literature had to have a social dimension; but it was precisely this social dimension which was denied to literature by the élitism which was a consequence of Aestheticism's preoccupation with the singularity of a writer's style. To argue for the aesthetic élitism of the kind proposed by these writers was therefore in itself a political act: for Swinburne, Pater and Wilde aesthetics was an engagement with politics, not an avoidance of them. However, according to one of Poggioli's central premises – the incompatibility of aesthetic and social radicalism[18] – this combination of features is impossible. Hence Poggioli's cryptic remark, 'the writer in England . . . tends . . . obscurely to confound . . . the problem of the avant-garde'.[19] Hence too his virtual exclusion of late nineteenth-century writers from his account of avant-gardism. Counter-examples such as these British writers would indeed overturn his whole theory.[20]

The problem in fact is not so much to do with the nature of the particular features which Poggioli describes as preconditions for avant-gardism, but with the lack of precision with which he uses them. Jones states this problem as follows:

> it is not always clear whether he [Poggioli] sees the 'artists' *works* revealing these characteristics, or whether they are supposed to be traits of the artists themselves, as men, ... This question is important since it issues in all the well-known ambiguities of failing to distinguish between an artist expressing *himself* in some way or other, his *work* expressing something, . . . or his work being seen as *expressive.*[21]

It is thus unclear how Poggioli's description of what the avant-garde *is* relates to what it *does*: to use Jones's example, is the artist alienated? Is the work alienated? – that is, does it exhibit alienation? And if so, how? Or is it itself alienated? If so, from what? Or, to use another concept of expressivity, does the work induce in the reader or spectator a state of alienation? The fundamental problem, then, with Poggioli's definition is its generality, a necessary consequence of his concern with a transhistorical definition which will accommodate all possible avant-gardes. In stipulating general conditions, Poggioli cannot account for the relationship of avant-garde movements to specific cultural issues; moreover he cannot account for the larger cultural and political functions of various avant-gardes. But Poggioli also debars himself from accounting for differences between avant-garde movements, since to do so would invalidate, or at least severely undermine, one of his fundamental premises – that avant-gardism (revealingly he uses the term 'the avant-garde') is a single recognisable phenomenon, about which it is possible to make generalisations. The price of this assumption is, of course, the exclusion of any example which does not immediately fit the generalisation – in particular those radical or innovative late nineteenth-century British artists and writers.

It is over precisely these issues – the failure to account for the political function of avant-garde movements and the generality of his theory – that Peter Bürger engages with Poggioli; Bürger's *Theory* is an attempt to describe the political function of avant-garde movements by locating them within their specific historical and cultural contexts. However, as I have already suggested, Bürger's theory is also an engagement with a long tradition of Marxist interest in avant-gardism. In order to fully appreciate Bürger's contribution to avant-garde theorising, it is necessary to set his work in the context of a specific tradition of German Marxist debate about aesthetics.

Marxism's interest in avant-gardism grew out of a debate about aesthetics which took place in Germany in the 1930s and 1950s, the protagonists in which were Georg Lukács, Theodor Adorno, Walter Benjamin, Bertolt Brecht and Ernst Bloch.[22] Perry Anderson has argued that this interest in art was prompted by a realisation that the revolutionary climate of the early 1920s had disappeared, and that it was no longer possible to locate the practical foundations for a revolutionary class consciousness within an analysis of the unique character of the proletariat's life-experience,[23] However, as Pauline Johnson suggests, this interest in art was not a turning away from politics, for the central task of Western Marxism's preoccupation with aesthetics was to locate in art an alternative mechanism for raising class consciousness. Marxism, she argues, must 'attempt to give an account of the ability of the art-work to change the recipient's thinking, . . . [it must] explain the emancipatory impact of the work of art'.[24] Avant-garde movements are the prime subject for such an enquiry precisely because they produce the one kind of art which is popularly credited with the overarching 'intention' – if not necessarily the achievement – of changing established opinions. It is precisely the oppositional attitudes of avant-garde movements *vis-à-vis* society which give them the potential to be critical and subversive, and so to 'raise consciousness'. However, historical materialism, in its unrevised form, can in fact say very little about the revolutionary function of avant-garde art because in that philosophy of history, by definition, all major social, political and structural changes are determined in the first instance by the economic base. All art, even avant-garde art, is unnecessary to these mechanisms. Hence one of the issues in these early Marxist debates was the elaboration of more sophisticated and subtle versions of historical materialism to take account of such objections.

In recent years the most influential of those critiques of Marx has been that of the French philosopher Louis Althusser; it gave impetus to the work of a number of literary and art critics who achieved popularity in the late 1970s and early 1980s.[25] Central to Althusser's critique of Marx is a redefinition of the concept of ideology; for Althusser, ideology is 'profoundly unconscious' in that it cannot be separated from, or tested against, everyday experience: 'in ideology men do express, not the relations between them and their conditions of existence, but *the way* they live the relation between them and their conditions of existence.'[26] However, the problem with this particularly inflexible concept of ideology is that it debars art from having any unique political function; as Johnson suggests, Althusser's theory is tantamount to saying that 'art teaches us nothing we don't already know.'[27] The consequence of Althusser's critique and the literary and art criticism which drew upon it, was once again – and with a new urgency – to call into question the political centrality of avant-garde movements, a situation which is reflected in the most recent Marxist accounts of avant-gardism.

The 1980s, then, have witnessed yet another debate among Marxist critics over the function of avant-garde art. On one side of this debate is the work of critics from the Budapest school (such as Agnes Heller and Ferenc Fehér) who attempt to reinstate the political function of avant-garde movements as part of a more general ambition to rescue an avant-garde politics for the future. On the other side is Peter Bürger, who has also sought to redefine the political function of avant-garde movements but in a manner which effectively denies that such a function is, or ever was, possible. For him, avant-garde politics are no longer viable in contemporary society; avant-gardism, in other words, is a dead body consigned to history.[28] Bürger's *Theory* can thus be seen as a renewed attempt to define the political function of avant-gardism; and as such it locates itself against both Poggioli and the tradition of avant-garde thought which Bürger himself represents, as well as the work of former Marxists such as Lukács and Adorno. A brief outline of the positions of these latter two critics will serve to finalise the context in which Bürger's ambitions are to be understood.

In *The Meaning of Contemporary Realism* Lukács mounted his famous defence of Realist literature on the grounds that its 'organicism' – its 'totalising perspective' – opposed the false, partial viewpoint of everyday life. Avant-garde works are rejected by him as a decadent degeneration from this ideal; their protest is only abstract, and lacks the historical perspective necessary for recognising the forces capable of overcoming capitalism. Hence Lukács's famous preference for Thomas Mann over Franz Kafka: 'modernism means not the enrichment, but the negation of art.'[29] Conversely Adorno defended the 'non-organic' nature of avant-garde art on the grounds that it severed itself from the totalising perspective promoted by the 'culture industry' in order to adapt people to the conditions of everyday life in capitalist society. In *Philosophy of Modern Music* Adorno defended the esoteric nature of Schoenberg's atonal music (which rendered correctly 'the antinominal character of the relationship between the particular and the general') against the popularity courted by Stravinsky's neo-classical appropriation of traditional forms – in, for example, his use of Pergolesi in the Pulcinella Suite.[30]

There are problems with both Lukács's and Adorno's theories, the most debilitating of which – for Marxism – are their inabilities to account satisfactorily for the revolutionary function of art. Briefly, in Lukács's argument, there is no explanation of how precisely Realism works; how, that is, – to use his terms – given that the partial 'fetishised' perspective of modern life is an inescapable fact, the reader can recognise in realism a 'totalising' outlook. On the other hand, Adorno explains Schoenberg's music as being 'in the process of pursuing its own inner logic . . . transformed more and more from something significant into something obscure – even to itself.'[31] If this is the case, then such modern music is debarred from having anything but the most limited audience, and thus it is debarred also from any significant political effect. For these reasons Bürger describes the theories of both Adorno and Lukács as being 'functionless'.[32] His *Theory* is an attempt, in the same Marxist tradition, to describe the 'real' function of avant-garde art. Bürger's insight, taken from Herbert Marcuse, is to see that the function of works of art is institutionally determined and historically and culturally specific. In its attempt to describe the function of avant-garde art more precisely, Bürger's *Theory* is an engagement with all 'functionless' definitions of avant-gardism: particularly with those of Lukács, Adorno and Poggioli and, as Jochan Schulte-Sasse has argued, also with deconstruction.[33]

Bürger's *Theory of the Avant-Garde* contains a description of the 'level of intention of historical avant-garde movements' and an account of various avant-garde movements – Dadaism, Surrealism, Futurism – 'at work'. His argument is that the intention of the historical avant-garde was defined in terms of a social praxis – the integration of art with life – an undertaking which had as its central objective the destruction of the bourgeois institution of art whose 'organic unity' denied to art the ability to intervene in social life. For Bürger, this enterprise became a possibility when the autonomy of the institution of art was first exposed (though not attacked) by the works of Aestheticism. Bürger sees all subsequent avant-gardes as a response to Aestheticism's challenge. However, he goes on to argue that although the historical avant-garde 'made clear the significance art as an institution has for the effect of individual works', and that it thereby brought art into 'a new relationship to reality'.[34] Nevertheless avant-garde movements ultimately failed to achieve the total return of art to the praxis of life because, paradoxically, 'it is art as an institution that determines the measure of political effect avant-garde works have, and that art in bourgeois society continues to be a realm that is distinct from the praxis of life.'[35] It is this pessimism which leads Jochan Schulte-Sasse to suggest that in the end Bürger partially returns to the position of Lukács and Adorno. In Schulte-Sasse's reading of Bürger, the destruction of the institution of art in bourgeois society can only be achieved by decisive, extra-artistic structural changes. Indeed Bürger says of 'post-avant-garde art' that 'it can either resign itself to its autonomous status or "organize happenings" to break through that status. But without surrendering its claim to truth, art cannot simply deny the autonomy status and pretend that it has a direct effect.'[36]

Bürger attempts to solve the problem of the vexed relationship between aesthetic radicalism and political radicalism by arguing that the oppositional politics of avant-garde art is not apparent at the level of style or content, but rather it is manifest at the level of the work's *status*:

> The European avant-garde movements can be defined as an attack on the status of art in bourgeois society. What is negated is not an earlier form of art (a style) but art as an institution that is unassociated with the life praxis of men. When the avant-gardistes demanded that art become practical once again, they do not mean that the contents of works of art should be socially significant. The demand is not raised at the level of the contents of individual works. Rather, it directs itself to the way art functions in society, a process that does as much to determine the effect that works have as does the particular content.[37]

The attack by avant-garde movements on the status of art in bourgeois society is manifest in the negation of the concept 'work of art' (understood to mean an *organic* work of art); for it is the negation of 'the relationship between part and whole that characterizes the organic work of art' which allows the possibility of art's intervention in social life.[38] However, the question which Bürger's account begs is the manner in which avant-garde works, considered as *art*, achieve this negation. In other words, what is the relationship between the 'features' which characterise avant-garde art and its function. There are in fact only two features of avant-garde art which Bürger convincingly identifies as subversive of 'organic' art: 'montage' and 'collage'. But there is a great deal of art and literature (and we should note here that Bürger's theory only adequately accounts for the visual arts) which we would wish to call avant-garde which possesses neither of these features. Like Poggioli's *Theory*, Bürger's thesis is viciously circular: by defining avant-gardism in terms of a normative function he can only characterise as avant-garde those works which can be seen to fulfil that function. In such a view the aesthetic qualities of the work will only be important in so far as they contribute to that function: thus the aesthetic is always affiliated to the political. The limitations of Bürger's functional theory can clearly be seen when it is applied to movements such as Imagism and Vorticism. Both these avant-garde movements were closely related – they had members in common, they shared many aesthetic goals and one partly grew out of the other.[39] However, according to Bürger's criteria *only* Vorticism can be authentically avant-garde; for Vorticism defined itself in terms of cultural opposition (that is, in terms broadly similar to the desire for social praxis which Bürger describes) while Imagism defined itself simply in terms of a set of literary features. The problem, then, with Bürger's thesis is that which I outlined in the Introduction – defining avant-gardism in terms of a work's function necessarily inhibits what is to be said about the features of that work.

There is, moreover, a second general problem with defining avant-gardism in terms of a political function which Bürger's *Theory* also fails to overcome. The fact that political functions can only be fully perceived and defined with hindsight (or in retrospect) leads to some vexed questions concerning intention. Bürger's proposal has the effect of erasing the artist from the picture, for as the political consequences of the work take on an overriding importance, so the 'intention' of the artist becomes virtually irrelevant. This leads to an obvious contradiction: on the one hand a notion of intention is invoked in order to support the idea of the self-conscious revolutionary artist; but on the other, it is ignored for the purposes of explaining the political function of the work in question. Bürger states the problem as follows:

> the *intended purpose or function* of the avant-gardiste manifestation is most difficult to define. . . . The avant-gardiste artists counter . . .

functionlessness not by an art that would have consequences within the existing society, but rather by the principle of the sublation of art in the praxis of life. But such a conception makes it impossible to define the intended purpose of art. For an art that has been reintegrated into the practice of life, not even the absence of a social purpose can be indicated. . . . When art and the praxis of life are one, when the praxis is aesthetic and art is practical, art's purpose can no longer be discovered, because the existence of two distinct spheres (art and the praxis of life) that is constitutive of the concept of purpose or intended use has come to an end.[40]

In fact this problem derives from Bürger's attempt to explain the 'intended purpose or function of the avant-garde' solely in terms of the 'institution of art' – in terms of the mechanisms of its production, reception and distribution. As Ferenc Fehér has argued, an institutional theory can only partially account for such procedures because institutions are rule-bound and commerce with art is not: art is 'institutional and non-institutional in character at the same time, throughout its whole history'.[41] It is precisely the 'intention' of the artist which is most difficult to account for comprehensively in any institutional terms.

The most debilitating limitations of Bürger's particular functional theory, however, occur with his characterisation of Aestheticism. The Aesthetic movement is central to Bürger's historicising of avant-gardism; in his view it marks the decisive break in history which makes possible the subsequent critique of the institution of art and the attempted 'sublation' of art into the 'praxis of life' by the historical avant-garde. Bürger argues that prior to Aestheticism, although the institution of art was fully developed, within it there still 'functioned' works of art whose 'contents [were] of [a] thoroughly political character'. (The examples Bürger gives of such politicised art are Voltaire's *Contes* and Mallarmé's poems.) Aestheticism, in contrast, marked the point when 'the contents [of art] also lose their political character and art wants to be nothing other than art'. According to Bürger, it is precisely this depoliticisation of the content of the work of art – the revelation in the works of Aestheticism of the 'social ineffectuality' of art – which makes possible the subsequent 'self-criticism of the social subsystem that is art' by the historical avant-garde.[42] However, this characterisation of Aestheticism is simply incorrect. The work of Aestheticism (as that movement developed in Britain) did *not* 'lose its political character'. As I have briefly indicated (and will discuss fully in later chapters) the work of that movement was thoroughly engaged with contemporary social and political issues.[43] It was precisely because the contents of Aesthetic works of art were never considered to be 'nothing other than art' that writers such as Swinburne, Pater and Wilde were so vilified. This mischaracterisation of Aestheticism by Bürger is a serious problem for his theory as a whole for, if I am correct, then the distinction which Bürger draws between Voltaire, Mallarmé and Aestheticism no longer holds; hence Bürger's claim for the significance of Aestheticism as the necessary precondition for avant-garde activity is not plausible. Neither is the characterisation of an avant-garde whose existence depends upon the uniqueness of Aestheticism.[44] The problem arises from Bürger's failure to define what and whom he means by the Aesthetic Movement and the doctrine of 'art for art's sake'. It is unclear, for example, exactly what kind of phenomenon Aestheticism was – it was certainly not a coherent movement in the sense of a shared political perspective. As many critics have been quick to point out, the adherents of the doctrine 'art for art's sake' had widely disparate political views.[45] It becomes very difficult, in other words, to attribute to these scattered individuals, who are connected by anything but their politics, the kind of agency which Bürger's *Theory* seems to suggest.

It is possible to draw several conclusions, both general and particular, from Bürger's and Poggioli's attempts to theorise avant-gardism. First, it is clear that both their definitions of avant-gardism are tautologous: what is to count as avant-garde is determined by a prior decision, based on evaluative (rather than descriptive) aesthetic or political criteria, to decide which artists and writers comprise the 'authentic' avant-garde. Bürger's and Poggioli's theories, and the two traditions of avant-garde theorising which they represent, indicate that the label 'avant-garde' is a contested concept, and that the disagreements over definitions of the term exist at the level of aesthetic and political value judgements. In this respect it is not really surprising that adjudication between these two theories of avant-gardism has rarely been conducted at a theoretical level – that of 'theory qua theory'. That is, there has been no sustained attempt to examine these theories in terms of their relative coherence or plausibility; nor have they been 'tested' in terms of their ability to account for the exceptional example – such as those oppositional artists and writers in late nineteenth-century Britain. Because there is no agreement about the nature of avant-gardism – about the object which each theory purports to explain – there can be no possible grounds for a proper adjudication between either account. It does not, therefore, seem unreasonable to suggest that the marginalisation of British artists and writers has been due simply to a failure of theory: the omission in avant-garde histories of figures such as Pater, Swinburne and Wilde (and to a lesser extent, William Morris) has been largely because their inclusion would radically controvert existing definitions of avant-gardism. To take proper account of the radicalism of such writers would involve a wholesale redefinition of the accepted views of avant-gardism – a task which few critics would be willing to undertake. So the oppositional British writers and artists who do not easily fit existing definitions of avant-gardism – because they cannot be categorised as simply aesthetic radicals or political radicals (however these terms are defined) – have simply been neglected. However, as I have briefly indicated, there were significant political and aesthetic concerns in the work of Pater, Swinburne and Wilde; their preoccupation with style did not mean that politics were not an issue for them, nor did it mean that political concerns are absent from their work. Rather, in their work the relationship between the aesthetic and the political is both more vexed and more complex, and hence it requires a more sophisticated theory of avant-gardism – one sensitive to the interrelationships between aesthetics and politics – to account for their oppositional strategies.

A new theory of avant-gardism which claims to account for the British example without marginalising other avant-gardes must be based upon some property or feature, however basic, which *all* avant-garde movements share; it must be able to account for British oppositional artists and writers in exactly the same terms as other more familiar European avant-gardes. An understanding of the nature and degree of British 'difference' is a necessary first step to finding just such a property. But one possibility has to be investigated first. Given the striking absence of nineteenth-century British artists and writers from histories and theories of the avant-garde, it is possible that Britain was unique, isolated from the continent – that there are no activities in Britain comparable to those, say, of the avant-garde movements in late nineteenth-century France, simply because events on the continent did not happen in Britain. However, at a practical level, this explanation seems inherently unlikely. The relationship between Britain and the continent – especially France, where cultural avant-gardism is generally supposed to have originated – was probably more intimate in the late nineteenth century than at any previous time. Indeed, there is a whole body of cultural criticism devoted to exploring Anglo-French relations, prompted by the impressive number of British artists and writers who spent large amounts of time in France and assiduously promoted continental ideas on their return to Britain; Swinburne's championing of Baudelaire and Hugo was just one example among many.[46] (There is a further element to this argument which I shall consider in more detail below. It suggests that while Britain was not unaware of life beyond the Channel, continental ideas were never able to take root in Britain because of its peculiarly conservative intellectual climate. This argument holds the view that as the dominant intellectual climate in Britain was hostile to certain kinds of ideas, they could only be entertained in a modified form and in covert ways. Such an explanation of British 'difference' retains a notion of uniqueness in terms of some degree of insularity, but does not rule out the possibility of outside influences.)

A second reason for the marginalisation of oppositional British artists and writers may be the apparent absence of any formal statement of their polemic. The usual view of avant-gardism (be it 'political' or 'aesthetic') maintains that the clearest statement of avant-garde polemic is to be found in the collective manifestos which avant-garde movements produced for the purpose of propagandising their theories of art. Thus Harold Rosenberg argues that:

> the key [to the avant-garde] is the ideological community, that is to say, a collective movement based upon certain intellectual presuppos- itions. An individual can be an innovator, but there is no such thing as an avant-garde individual, except as follower or leader.[47]

A typical statement by such an intellectual community would be the manifestos produced by Imagism in 1914 and 1915. However, in late nineteenth-century Britain, movements such as Aestheticism produced no comparable collective public statement about their theories of art (a situation which led Poggioli to claim that there was an absence of avant-garde theorising in Britain at this time). Indeed, as I have indicated, historians of Aestheticism have frequently drawn attention to the disparate and incoherent nature of the writing produced by the various members of that 'movement'.[48] Neverthe- less it is the case that despite the polemic of Aestheticism being expressed in scattered individual statements which rarely cohered into any single theory, that polemic was still popularly believed to derive from a movement, from, in Rosenberg's terms, an ideological community. The anonymous reviewer in the *British Quarterly* in 1882 would have been exactly understood when he or she referred to Aestheticism in this manner:

> a movement supported by an influential and, it must be owned, an educated party, and led by men of considerable talent, and it is just now in a proselytising humour, and appears to be making way among people who do not clearly recognise what they are following.[49]

Indeed it was precisely the perception that the members of the Aesthetic movement (or the Pre-Raphaelite Brotherhood before it) were a highly cohesive group which caused alarm and provoked allegations that they were a coterie or élite. To all intents and purposes, then, British oppositional artists and writers were not substantially different from their continental contemporaries; there was in Britain a great deal of radical polemic and a great deal of sophisticated and subtle theorising about art. However, the polemic of late nineteenth-century British oppositional writers is to be found in a different discourse, that of literary criticism. It exists, for example, in the 'Conclusion' to Pater's *Renaissance*, in Swinburne's essays on William Blake and George Chapman, and in Wilde's *Intentions*. It was by means of discussing the work of other artists and writers that figures such as Swinburne, Pater and Wilde articulated their own theories of art, and thus covertly defended their own artistic practices. Hence it is the *form* in which their polemic appeared which marks off British oppositional writers as different. Why should this have happened? Why did writers, so well versed with the activities of their French counterparts, choose a form so circumspect as literary criticism to propound their views? For the conventions which governed the publication of literary criticism – the informal powers of censorship, of the periodical press and so forth – naturally put constraints both on what could be said and how it could be said. The answer lies in the profound intellectual conservatism, alluded to above, which characterised nineteenth-century Britain. I shall describe the nature of this conservatism and the forms it took in more detail in the following chapter; here it is sufficient to notice that this conservatism, which might have suppressed oppositional writing completely in Britain, only ensured that political and artistic dissent had to be disguised by, or contained within, conventional forms.[50]

Clearly an ability to take account of national cultural and intellectual specificities must, as Bürger recognised, be an important component of a 'useful' theory of avant-gardism: otherwise British 'difference' cannot be explained. However, it is the argument of this book that the most basic way of understanding avant-gardism is not in terms of a specific function, nor in terms of a set of features or aspects, but rather in terms of a *relationship*: all avant-garde movements – literary, artistic, architectural, or otherwise – define themselves in relation to the past – *to tradition*. To be innovative, to be ahead of one's time, implies some kind of disavowal both of 'what is' – the status quo – and what has been – tradition. Moreover, as I have suggested, what is at issue is not the degree of this disavowal (whether or not, for example, avant-gardism depends upon a total repudiation of the past and a totally hostile attitude towards society) but the form which it takes. The form of that opposition to the past is itself determined to a large extent by the singularity of the intellectual and cultural climate in which the avant-garde artist or writer is situated. Specifically, it is the general attitude within a culture towards the past which influences how avant-garde artists and writers define themselves in relation to tradition, and also, therefore, the manner and extent to which they repudiate those traditions.

It is clear that recent intellectual history can provide a useful model for such a theory of avant-gardism. It is a premiss of this intellectual history that particular intellectual changes can only be fully understood within the general ideational context of the society of which they are a part. Thus changes which are observed in literary and artistic practices – in this case the appearance of an avant-garde – cannot be explained solely in terms of the 'art-world' (however it is defined), as if such a world existed in isolation from other forms of intellectual activity. A general set of conditions has to be available to artists and writers in order for any artistic activity – including avant-garde opposition – to become a possibility. In the case of avant-gardism, these conditions include a concept of historical change (particularly the idea of starting afresh after a complete rupture with the past), and the belief that the individual can act independently without any recourse to traditional models of authority. However, the existence of these concepts, or something very like them, only provides the necessary preconditions for an 'ideal-type' of avant-garde activity to occur (in so far as notions of opposition and repudiation are inconceivable without them). Moreover, these conditions must precede – in the sense that they make possible – what avant-garde movements actually do. The literary critic or historian must look further to the general intellectual climate in which the individual artist or writer is situated in order to see whether and in what ways these conditions existed. Such a project approximates a sociology of knowledge; it involves a close examination of various disciplines of knowledge, including a consideration of the intellectual authority or prestige enjoyed by them. For it is only the interrelationships and the interdependence of a number of different disciplines, in turn determined by knowledge of the relative authority each discipline enjoyed, which can account for the kind of intellectual orthodoxies which circumscribe both the nature and form of avant-garde activity.

As I have indicated, in Britain such disciplines included political economy, sociology and historiography. The significance of historiography to discussions of the formation of avant-garde movements is most easy to see; the primary concern of history is with the meaning and relevance of past events for the present; in this sense, then, historiography 'creates' those traditions against which an avant-garde defines itself. Sociology is important also in so far as it uses and promotes the concepts developed by historiography, for history influences how the state of society – sociology's subject-matter – is to be perceived. For example, a sociology based upon the premises of an evolutionary history has quite different concerns from a sociology based upon a theory of revolutionary change. Finally, political economy is included for my specific historical concerns: in nineteenth-century Britain its explanatory power (as I shall describe later) gave it the status of an ideology. The emphasis on individualism and the popularity of *laissez-faire* politics made political economy instrumental in maintaining the intellectual conservatism which I suggest characterised many aspects of British intellectual life. Indeed, as I have said, it is exactly the profoundly conservative nature of its intellectual climate which marks Britain out as different.[51] A precise account of the political strategies of late nineteenth-century British oppositional writers has to take into consideration these national intellectual constraints.

The approach to avant-gardism suggested here differs in several important ways from the theories discussed above. The most important of these differences concerns the nature of the explanations it can offer. This approach is more specific than Poggioli's *The Theory of the Avant-Garde* in that it can account very precisely for the historical and cultural uniqueness of different avant-garde movements; and it is more comprehensive than Bürger's *Theory of the Avant-Garde* in that its attention to the 'cultural context' encompasses a much wider area than that associated with the institution of art – with its production, reception, distribution, and so forth. Moreover, such an approach, as I have argued in my Introduction, is also underwritten by a set of assumptions concerning the relationships between diverse disciplines of knowledge. At one level, it merely assumes the obvious: that artists and writers, in nineteenth-century Britain especially, were surrounded by a complex network of ideas, and that their work ought to be seen as part of, and therefore inevitably engaged with, larger intellectual issues. However, where this approach is innovative is in its ability to supply a mechanism – a concept of intellectual authority – whereby the connections between literary and artistic practices and the ideational context in which they are situated may be established very precisely. The methodology proposed here allows the critic to be confident in determining exactly which particular ideas within that complex network were responsible for bringing about, or for influencing, certain kinds of literary and artistic forms.

Approaching avant-gardism in this way necessarily sets objectives quite distinct from those of Poggioli and Bürger. First, it assumes a certain provisionality about the concept of avant-gardism itself, an acknowledgement that it is a *post hoc* explanation. Because there is such a diversity between the strategies adopted by various avant-garde movements, it makes little sense to refer to 'the avant-garde' as if it were a transcultural or transhistorical phenomenon. At best there are various avant-gardes, modifications of an ideal type of avant-garde activity: avant-gardism can only have necessary, but never sufficient, conditions.[52] To borrow some observations from Quentin Skinner, when it comes to considering avant-gardism 'there are only individual answers to individual questions, with as many different answers as there are questions, and as many different questions as there are questioners'.[53] If, then, the concept of avant-gardism is only to be a heuristic tool, it also follows that there can be no simple, authentic history of the avant-garde, nor indeed any single comprehensive theory of it. The most that may be allowed is a history of one particular avant-garde – the British, French or whatever – which is nationally specific; and then an account, based upon close attention to the specificities of the intellectual and cultural climate, of the strategies of opposition to the past developed by the particular avant-garde movement in question. Hence the intentionally and necessarily limited scope of this book – it is an attempt to account only for the late nineteenth-century British literary avant-garde.

The final advantage of the approach to avant-gardism which I have proposed is that it is capable of overcoming the general problems of avant-garde theorising outlined at the beginning of this chapter. Fundamentally, it solves the problem posed by the existence of two different avant-garde canons, the political and the aesthetic. By dissolving the opposition between the categories of the political and the aesthetic, the approach I propose naturally invalidates judgements based upon those distinctions. Hence Courbet can be considered no more 'effectively' nor 'authentically' avant-garde than, say, Flaubert or Pater. Such an approach also solves the problem of accurately dating cultural avant-gardism: avant-garde movements are seen as evolving at a particular point in time and as a reaction to the particular intellectual and cultural climate in which they are situated; and they possess a uniquely national character. Viewing avant-gardism in this way makes it possible to be more faithful and sensitive to history, for the political activities of different avant-garde movements may be described without resorting to anachronistic evaluations or to simplistic oppositions between aesthetic and political radicalism. My account of avant-gardism does not castigate artists for failing in a task that they may not have intended to complete, but instead describes their projects in the context of the particular intellectual environments in which they worked, evaluating them in their own and their contemporaries' terms, rather than in ours.

Notes

1. Linda Nochlin, *Gustave Courbet: A study of style and society* (New York: Garland, 1976).
2. Ibid. 227.
3. Linda Nochlin, 'The invention of the avant-garde in France, 1830–80'

in Thomas B. Hess and John Ashbery (eds.), *The Avant-Garde, Art News Annual*, 34 (1968), 16.

4. Donald Drew Egbert, 'The idea of the "avant-garde" in art and politics', *American Historical Review*, 73 (1967), 339–66.

5. Indeed Nochlin's failure to engage critically with a concept of avant-gardism which is clearly inadequate, and her tendency instead to transfer the inadequacy to the artist or writer in question, is not unusual.

6. Charles Rosen and Henri Zerner, *Romanticism and Realism: The mythology of nineteenth-century art* (London: Faber and Faber, 1984), 133–79. See also Gabriel P. Weisberg, *The Realist Tradition: French painting and drawing 1830–1900* (Cleveland, Ohio: Cleveland Museum of Art, 1980).

7. Rosen and Zerner, 160, 161.

8. See for example: Donald Drew Egbert, *Social Radicalism and the Arts: Western Europe* (London: Duckworth, 1970); and George Woodcock, *Anarchism* (Harmondsworth: Penguin, 1963) and *The Paradox of Oscar Wilde* (London: T. V. Boardman, 1949).

9. See, for example, Richard Dellamora, *Masculine Desire* (Chapel Hill and London: University of North Carolina Press, 1990).

10. See the Introduction to Ian Small and Russell Jackson (eds.), *Oscar Wilde, Two Society Comedies* (London: Ernest Benn, 1983).

11. An exception to this is John Weightman, *The Concept of the Avant-Garde* (London: Alcove Press, 1973), who suggests a distinction, based on cultural differences, between French and British avant-gardes. However, his explanation is highly unconvincing, comprising an idiosyncratic and tautologous definition of avant-gardism – that of nineteenth-century artists' preoccupation with time, deriving from an evolutionary rather than cyclical view of time itself.

12. It should be noted that the history of avant-garde movements is not the same as the history of modernism. In the past, especially in the United States, these two concepts – modernism and avant-garde – have tended to be used interchangeably and this has led to considerable confusion.

13. See Egbert, ibid. Peter Bürger, *Theory of the Avant-Garde* (Manchester: Manchester University Press, 1984) is an exception in this tradition. In his theory the first authentic avant-garde does not appear until the early twentieth century. The problems with Bürger's dating will be discussed separately below.

14. See, for example, Matei Calinescu, *Faces of Modernity: Avant-Garde, Decadence, Kitsch* (Bloomington, Indiana: Indiana University Press, 1977).

15. Egbert, *Social Radicalism*, 717.

16. See Peter Jones's review of Poggioli's *The Theory of the Avant-Garde* in the *British Journal of Aesthetics*, 9 (1969), 87.

17. This has been a common thread between George Woodcock's discussion of Wilde's anarchism and, more recently, Regenia Gagnier's account of Wilde's engagement with an emerging consumerist culture. See George Woodcock, *The Paradox of Oscar Wilde* (op. cit.) and Regenia Gagnier,

Idylls of the Market Place: Oscar Wilde and the Victorian public (Aldershot: Scolar, 1987).

18. Poggioli argued that their alliance was 'theoretically and historically erroneous'. See Poggioli, *The Theory of the Avant-Garde*, 95.
19. Ibid. 8.
20. Poggioli's book has one passing reference to Wilde and none at all to Pater. Oddly it is the nonsense verse of Edward Lear which is afforded most attention in Poggioli's account of nineteenth-century British avant-gardism.
21. Jones, 87.
22. See Ernst Bloch, Georg Lukács, Bertolt Brecht, Walter Benjamin and Theodor Adorno, *Aesthetics and Politics*, ed. and trans., Ronald Taylor (London: Verso, 1977).
23. Perry Anderson, *Considerations on Western Marxism* (London: New Left Books, 1978).
24. Pauline Johnson, *Marxist Aesthetics* (London: Routledge and Kegan Paul, 1984), 5.
25. The influence of Althusser can be seen, for example, in the work of recent British critics such as Catherine Belsey and Terry Eagleton, and also in Pierre Macherey, *A Theory of Literary Production*, trans. Geoffrey Wall (London: Routledge and Kegan Paul, 1978).
26. L. Althusser, 'Marxism and Humanism' in *For Marx* (London: Penguin, 1969), 223. Quoted in Johnson, 117–18.
27. Johnson, 126.
28. See Ferenc Fehér and Agnes Heller (eds.), *Reconstructing Aesthetics* (Oxford: Basil Blackwell, 1986); Peter Bürger, op. cit.; and Andreas Huyssen, 'The hidden dialectic: avant-garde – technology – mass culture' in *After The Great Divide: Modernism, mass culture and postmodernism* (London: Macmillan, 1988), 3–15.
29. Georg Lukács, *The Meaning of Contemporary Realism* (London: Merlin Press, 1972), 46.
30. Theodor Adorno, *Philosophy of Modern Music* (London: Sheed and Ward, 1973).
31. Ibid. 19.
32. It ought to be noted in passing that Bürger defines an artistic function in a special and limited way. See Bürger, 10–14.
33. Schulte-Sasse argues that a 'text-theory' such as deconstruction does not allow to art and literature any practical intervention into capitalist society. See Jochan Schulte-Sasse, 'Foreword: Theory of modernism versus theory of the avant-garde' in Bürger, op. cit., vii–xlvii.
34. Bürger, 90, 91.
35. Ibid. 92.
36. Ibid. 57.
37. Ibid. 49.
38. Ibid. 56.
39. For a discussion of the relationship between Imagism and Vorticism see William C. Wees, *Vorticism and the English Avant-Garde* (Manchester: Manchester University Press, 1972); and Richard Cork, *Vorticism and*

Abstract Art in the First Machine Age, 2 vols. (London: Gordon Fraser, (eds.) 1976).
40. Bürger, 51.
41. Ferenc Fehér, 'What is beyond art?' in Fehér and Heller (eds.), op. cit., 65. Besides Fehér, there have been many other criticisms of the institutional theory of art. See in particular: R'chard Wollheim, 'The institutional theory of art' in *Art and its Objects* (2nd edn, Cambridge: Cambridge University Press, 1980), 157–66; and Robert McGregor, 'Dickie's institutionalized aesthetic', *British Journal of Aesthetics*, 17 (1977), 3–13.
42. Bürger, 26.
43. Regenia Gagnier has also criticised Bürger's characterisation of Aestheticism. She argues:

> Late Victorian aestheticism was not the divorce between life and art that Gautier's phrase *l'art pour l'art* may suggest. Beyond Bürger's Weberian sphere of 'art-world', I would propose a theory of aestheticism from the point of view of consumption, or of the different public that, in different ways, consumed it. Ultimately, I locate the interrelations of art world and life world in the practices of modern spectacular society.

Gagnier illustrates her argument by reference to Wilde's play, *The Importance of Being Earnest*. She suggests that 'far from being autonomous, *Earnest* as performance negates those determinations that are essential in autonomous art . . . [;] the performance merges with the audience, thus obliterating the distinction of art from life.' See Gagnier, op. cit., 6–7, 8.
44. Peter Uwe Hohendahl has also criticised Bürger's periodisation, arguing that 'the avant-garde . . . continues to rely on the romantic paradigm of sublation and with it the concept of aesthetic autonomy.' See Peter Uwe Hohendahl, 'The Loss of Reality: Gottfried Benn's early prose' in Andreas Huyssen and David Bathrick (eds.), *Modernity and the Text* (New York: Columbia University Press, 1989), 81–94.
45. See, for example, R. V. Johnson, *Aestheticism* (London: Methuen, 1969); and Ian Small, *The Aesthetes* (London: Routledge and Kegan Paul, 1979).
46. For a recent example of this interest see, Ceri Crossley and Ian Small (eds.), *Studies in Anglo-French Cultural Relations* (London: Macmillan, 1988); and Patricia Clements, *Baudelaire and the English Tradition* (Princeton, N.J.: Princeton University Press, 1985).
47. Harold Rosenberg, 'Collective, ideological, combative' in *Art News Annual*, op. cit., 75.
48. See, for example, R. V. Johnson, 9–13.
49. Unsigned Review, 'Art V: The poetry of Rossetti', *British Quarterly*, 76 (1882), 109.
50. In fact there are two aspects to the use of literary critical discourses by oppositional British writers. Not only did they use this medium to voice their challenge to literary and artistic orthodoxies, but they also

simultaneously subverted the conventions which governed the practice of literary criticism. This second process of subversion centred on their undermining of conventional mechanisms of intellectual authority; it concerns their eclectic and complex use of devices such as quotation, citation and allusion. This topic has been addressed in detail by Ian Small. See Ian Small, *Conditions for Criticism: Authority, knowledge and literature in the late nineteenth century* (Oxford: Clarendon Press, 1991).

51. In characterising the British intellectual climate as highly conservative, I am referring mainly to the conservatism exhibited by those disciplines which have most effect on avant-garde activities – sociology, historiography and political economy. There were, of course, other areas of debate in Britain at this time – particularly those concerning religion – for which the term conservative may seem inappropriate. However, while these debates may have influenced individual writers and artists, they were not part of the necessary conditions – the problematising of concepts of society and history – which make avant-garde activities possible.

52. It might be objected at this point that in defining avant-gardism in terms of an 'ideal-type' I am still offering an essentialist definition, and that I have not therefore made any real advance on those theories by other critics. However, the essentialist definition put foward in this book does have one very significant difference; it does not claim to be a sufficient definition of avant-gardism. The proposal that all avant-gardes define themselves in terms of some form of opposition to the past, or to tradition, will alone tell us very little about individual artists and writers. The specificity of particular avant-garde movements will only be revealed on a further examination of the individual intellectual conditions which produced that movement. It is impossible to make any useful generalisations about these conditions – impossible, that is, to define them in essentialist terms. Avant-gardism, in other words, requires a special kind of essentialist definition, one which is accompanied by a series of qualifying conditions.

53. Quentin Skinner, 'Meaning and understanding in the history of ideas', *History and Theory*, 8 (1969), 50.

CHAPTER 3

The conditions for avant-garde activity in nineteenth-century Britain

In the previous chapter I argued that avant-garde movements define themselves in relation to the past – to tradition. I further suggested that the manner and extent to which they repudiate traditions are determined by the general attitudes within a culture towards the past. Ideal conditions for avant-garde activity occur in an intellectual climate where both a concept of historical rupture and a belief that the individual can act without recourse to traditional models of authority are readily available to artists and writers – conditions which occurred, for example, in post-Revolutionary France. However, in nineteenth-century Britain the intellectual climate was characterised by a deep conservatism which was hostile to these ideas. The result was that conditions for avant-garde activity were quite different in Britain. My intention in this chapter is to describe these conditions more exactly by examining the disciplines of knowledge – historiography and sociology – which had (and have) most influence in shaping attitudes within a culture towards the past.

The emphasis which I shall give to the distinctiveness of late nineteenth-century British avant-garde movements runs counter to the tendency, common for the past forty years or so, to describe Aestheticism, Symbolism and Decadence almost exclusively in terms of French origins and models.[1] This view is based on the assumption that the transfer of ideas between France and Britain in the late nineteenth century was relatively straightforward; and at a superficial level, the ready commerce which certain British artists and writers had with France at this time may appear to lend support to it.[2] However, it has recently been argued that the general processes of Franco-British acculturation were complex and restricted, and that the manner in which one country appropriates the ideas of another can be highly problematic. In the first place, foreign ideas can rarely be adopted *tout court*; they invariably have to be adapted to fit the demands of the adopting culture; and in the second, different disciplines within that culture are able to 'use' these ideas in different ways.[3] The difficulties encountered by British 'borrowers' from France in the nineteenth century occurred because of the quite different intellectual traditions at work in the two countries. In general terms, there was a fundamental opposition between on the one hand, a French tradition of rationalist and monistic thought – which tended to be deductive in method and whose model of authority was the Catholic Church – and, on the other, a British tradition of empiricism, inductive in method, whose model of authority was the individual.[4] It seems reasonable to suppose (at least until it can be disproved) that if intellectual differences affected developments in disciplines such as historiography and sociology in Britain and France, then they also affected developments in art and literature. It is clear that writers such as Swinburne, Pater, Morris and Wilde found themselves as circumscribed as their contemporaries in other areas of intellectual activity when it came to making use of French ideas. My argument, then, is not to deny altogether the influence of French ideas but to stress that interest in them was coupled with a perception of their inappropriateness to a British context; these ideas could be employed in Britain only in modified forms and in covert ways. Therefore, it is mistaken to assume that the ambitions of British avant-garde artists and writers were analogous to those of their French counterparts and mistaken also to conclude that British avant-garde projects were by comparison very timid, no more than late and faded flowerings of more vigorous French predecessors. Rather it is the case that the conditions for avant-garde activity were quite different in Britain, and that British avant-gardes adopted strategies of opposition to the past which were suited to the peculiarities of their own intellectual climate. One of the advantages of viewing the polemic of British avant-gardes in this way is that it rescues them from marginalisation, for when seen as an attack on specifically *British* institutions and intellectual orthodoxies, their projects are revealed to be no less subversive and no less provocative than those of their better-known European relations.

The first significant contrast between intellectual conditions in Britain and in France occurs in the area of historiography. The most decisive event in shaping attitudes towards the past and towards the authority of tradition in the nineteenth century was the French Revolution. The Revolution suggested that it was indeed possible to repudiate the authority of tradition and to sweep away all that had gone before. As one nineteenth-century historian cogently argued, 'cette révolution n'a pas seulement modifié le pouvoir politique, elle a changé toute l'existence intérieure de la nation.'[5] The confident repudiation of tradition which is characteristic of much French avant-gardism can be explained both in terms of the availability of this 'revolutionary heritage' and of its relatively unproblematic nature. Two striking examples of the different ways in which this heritage could be appropriated for artistic programmes are to be found in the work of Gustave Courbet and Edouard Manet.

Courbet's most subversive works, his Realist paintings of the early 1850s, exhibit two debts to his revolutionary heritage. The first, and most often commented upon, is to the politics of the 1848 Revolution; Courbet's attempt to incorporate revolutionary proletarian and democratic ideals into an artistic programme, to create, that is, a new art divorced from all institutional apparatuses which would be of, and for, the people, clearly stemmed from the immediate political ambitions of his contemporaries at the barricades.[6] But Courbet also had a further and more general 'ideological' debt to the older 1789 myths of rupture and reconstruction. In his choice of subject matter – the common people – and the manner in which he portrayed it – using popular contemporary iconography – Courbet displayed a total disregard for the conventions of a whole tradition of history painting.[7] This aggressive assertion of the importance of the contemporary was, to borrow Joseph Sloane's phrase, nothing less that a 'declaration of war on the past'.[8] Manet's attitude towards tradition was rather more complex and ambiguous, although for his public it was no less provocative. During the first half of the nineteenth century the Venetian School had become very popular in France and pictorial allusions to it were common; one of the most famous was *The Romans and the Decadence* by Thomas Couture, Manet's teacher. However, Manet's own backward glance at Titian in his *Olympia*, and his recalling of Giorgione and Raphael in *Déjeuner sur l'herbe*, were greeted with extreme hostility or simply ignored because his use of these artists, far from revering them, appeared radically to question their authority.[9] Manet's transposition of Titian's domestic Venus into a worldly prostitute, and his introduction of contemporary figures – actually his mistress and some friends – into a Venetian-style landscape suggested the need to 'modernise' the Masters: like Venturi's modern National Gallery plans, tradition, if it was to maintain any relevance for the present, had to be accommodated to the demands of the contemporary artist. But this view completely overturned the orthodox use of tradition; it suggested that tradition, far from being the adjudicator, was itself to be judged.

Both Courbet and Manet defined themselves in relation to the art of the past, and both did so in a manner which suggested little respect for the authority of tradition. However, the differences in their attitudes suggest that the exact relationship between their Revolutionary heritage and the work which French avant-garde artists and writers produced is in fact a more complex subject than I have so far indicated.[10] In the first place it is clear that revolutionary ideologies were more easily assimilated into artistic programmes at some points in time than at others. Courbet worked fired by the optimism of the 1848 Revolution, but Manet's experience a decade and a half later was of what Michelet described as *les faits cruels* which followed the demise of the Second Republic. The possibilities which had been open to Courbet in the 1850s may then have appeared as distant and perhaps unrealisable ideals. (Indeed even Courbet's own works at this time were more conventional.) Second, there were also quite different ways in which a revolutionary heritage could be used. As I have indicated, Courbet's attempt to democratise art 'borrowed' from specific political ideologies of the 1848 Revolution; but his and Manet's rejection of the authority of tradition was indebted to the more general revolutionary myths of rupture and reconstruction.

While all of this is true, the strongest objection to my argument stated so far is likely to be the problem posed by the complexity of the revolutionary heritage itself. This was due not so much to its encompassing several different revolutions (1789, 1830, 1848 and 1871), but more to the fact that it embraced a very wide spectrum of opinion, ranging from Jules Michelet's romantic myth of the Revolution's populist origins at one end, to Alexis de Tocqueville's rigorous examination of the Revolution's democratic credentials at the other. French Revolutionary historiography is clearly too large and complex a subject to address here in any detail, but my argument in any case does not rest on the particular borrowings by avant-garde writers and artists from particular historians. Rather I am concerned with establishing the general intellectual trends or orthodoxies within a culture. At one level the sheer quantity of historical writing on the Revolution is itself testimony to the scale of the debate about the past, and its relevance to the present, all of which the Revolution provoked. As an irreducible minimum, the French Revolution problematised attitudes towards the past; and the attempt by avant-garde movements to redefine the relationship between the contemporary artist and tradition was only part of this much larger process of relocation. I want, however, to make a more specific claim than this: namely, that the dominant interpretation of the Revolution by the 'liberal' historians, the one which became virtually an orthodoxy in nineteenth-century France, established a radically new attitude towards the past and the authority of tradition which proved to be immensely liberating for avant-garde artists and writers.

The liberal interpretation of the Revolution was established in the 1820s by François Mignet and Adolphe Thiers. Their main political task during the Restoration was to offer to the French a sanitised account of the Revolution acquitted of its crimes, and to achieve this aim they located the Revolution within a specific liberal past, viewing it as the culmination of an uninterrupted tradition of French liberty. They then abstracted a revolutionary ideal from the crimes which had been committed in its name, and bequeathed it to the future as one 'purely conceived' but 'unfortunately corrupted'.[11] For my purposes, the two most significant features of this interpretation were as follows. First, there was the tendency to ignore or subordinate the activities of individuals and to portray the Revolution as if it were an abstract force following a predetermined course, so much so that 'la marche de la Révolution' became inevitable and inexorable. Second, there was a corresponding emphasis on the dramatic and inevitable break with the past which the Revolution effected; in the name of progress, revolution had the power, and the right, to sweep away all institutions, all laws and all moral imperatives which had existed before. In a recent essay Roger Scruton has suggested that revolutionary ideologies, including that of the French Revolution, are always negative in character; they sanction nothing but destruction. 'The effect of revolutionary ideology', he argues, 'is to introduce a kind of incurable nihilism into the social order, to infect all public processes with the sense that they are without justification, and to be understood merely as the passing drift of power.' ' "Liberty" ', he continues, 'since it denoted no achievable goal, came to refer to the purely *negative* principle that all powers on earth are powers of usurpation, and can therefore be destroyed.'[12] Mignet's introductory comments to his *Histoire* provide a cogent summary of the 'liberal perspective':

> En retracant l'histoire de cette importante période, depuis l'overture des états généraux jusqu'en 1814, je me propose d'expliquer les diverses crises de la révolution en même temps que j'en exposerai la marche. Nous verrons par la faute de qui, après s'être ouverte sous de si heureux auspices, elle dégénéra violemment; de quelle manière elle changea la France en république, et comment, sur les débris de celle-ci, elle éleva l'empire. Ces diverses phases ont été presque obligées, tant les événements qui les ont produites ont eu une irrésistible puissance! Il serait pourtant téméraire d'affirmer que la face des choses n'eut pas pu devenir différente; mais ce qu'il y a certain, c'est que la révolution, avec les causes qui l'ont amenée et les passions qu'elle a employées ou soulevées devait avoir cette marche et cette issue. . . . J'espère montrer . . . qu'il n'a guère été plus possible de l'éviter que de la conduire.[13]

This line of defence was modified only in subtle ways by subsequent historians: Michelet, for example, gave the abstract revolutionary force a distinctly dramatic national character: 'la Révolution est en nous, dans nos âmes' he argued, it is 'la grande âme commune . . . [qui] est comprisée par des peuples divers, et le sera par d'autres générations dans l'avenir.'[14] The argument itself underwent little substantial change throughout the nineteenth and early part of the twentieth century. Thus, in so far as it enjoyed a general currency during this period (Mignet's work was in its sixteenth edition in 1887) the liberal interpretation can be said to have provided the basic necessary conditions – the concepts of historical rupture and repudiation of tradition – for the development of avant-garde activity in France.[15]

The effect of the French Revolution in Britain was similar to that in France in so far as it also provoked, or rather renewed, a debate about the past. It led British historians to reflect anew upon the 'Glorious Revolution' of 1688 – specifically, upon the opposing interpretations of it by Burke, who had stressed constitutional continuity, and Hume, who had seen revolution as innovative and progressive. And at a more general level, the whole idea of revolutionary change and progress was discussed. However, the manner in which this British debate was resolved produced a situation which was almost diametrically opposed to that which had obtained in France. What emerged in Britain was a set of orthodoxies about the past, unchanged for most of the century, which were totally opposed to the ideas of historical rupture and repudiation of tradition which had been developed by French historians. These orthodoxies were apparent at one level in a common, non-partisan reaction by British historians to the French Revolution. Whig, Tory and Radical alike submerged their historical differences to share an attitude which reconciled the extremes of partiality and hostility: all tended to deny or ignore the novelty of the Revolution. In particular they were reluctant to acknowledge that it had indeed effected dramatic, decisive and beneficial changes in the structure of French society; and they all tended to view it as essentially a social or political revolt determined by 'crime and error'.[16] At another level, these orthodoxies were to be seen in the counter-assertion by most British historians of the importance of gradual change and respect for the authority of tradition; in their subscribing to the view of the past which came to dominate British historiography in the nineteenth century – Whiggish gradualism, with its combination of an idealisation of continuity with a faith in progress.[17] Hence, for example, the most popular historian of the first half of the century, Thomas Babington Macaulay, argued that the only conceivable, or supportable kind of revolution was one 'undertaken for the purpose of defending, correcting, and restoring – never for the mere purpose of destroying';[18] and he then famously described 'our revolution' – the 1688 Revolution – as:

> a vindication of ancient rights, so it was conducted with strict attention to ancient formalities. In almost every word and act may be discerned a profound reverence for the past. . . . Both the English parties agreed in treating with solemn respect the ancient constitutional traditions of the state. The only question was, in what sense those traditions were to be understood.[19]

James Mackintosh, too, could only endorse the idea of 'a defensive revolution' (such as 1688) 'of which the sole purpose is to preserve and secure the laws . . . and [which] is . . . exempt from the succession of changes which disturbs all habits of peaceable obedience, and weakens every authority not resting on mere force.'[20]

One of the principal reasons for the emergence of these orthodoxies was that British historians held quite different views about the nature of historical causation from their French counterparts. The main effect of the French Revolution on these views was negative, in that it made them become even more deeply entrenched. In other words, the hostility directed towards historians such as Mignet and Thiers was not simply on the grounds that they apparently condoned events which British historians wanted to condemn, but it was also because the whole nature of their interpretation of the past was seen to be dangerously subversive. Influenced by empiricist rather than rationalist traditions of thought, British historians saw causation as related to human, and invariably individual agency; they argued that because circumstances affect people in numerous ways, there cannot be a single process of causation, but only a number of causes, effects and futures. They were thus led to reject historiographies, such as those by Mignet and Thiers, which interpreted history in terms of ideas or abstract forces which underlay particular events and which suggested that there was a single overarching principle of historical change. In British eyes such histories appeared to be highly deterministic (and fatalistic) and, by ignoring the responsibility of human actants, they threatened to dispense with morality. The concepts of historical rupture and of the repudiation of tradition developed by French historians in order to interpret and understand the past were rejected in Britain not only as inappropriate to *British* history, but also as inappropriate to *history* – to historiography. This distinction, which I shall pick up later, accounts for the tenacity of gradualist, Whiggish historiography in Britain. Gradualism could not be superseded until the tenets of the entire discipline of historiography, with its empiricist methodology and philosophy, had been undermined. Such a situation did not begin to come about in Britain until the 1870s.

The implications of all this for British avant-garde movements are simple: in an intellectual climate where the concepts of historical rupture and repudiation of tradition had been comprehensively rejected, and where the dominant attitude towards the past was one which advocated historical continuity and a profound respect for tradition, there were virtually no conditions in which avant-garde activity could flourish.

The preconditions produced by historiography were essential to avant-garde activities: but so, too, in a less obvious way, were those produced by the discipline of sociology. Like historiography, sociology also problematised the concepts necessary for avant-garde activities. In its inception in the nineteenth century, the discipline of sociology was intimately related to historiography; sociological analyses of society proceeded from, and in turn helped to propagate, precisely those attitudes towards the past which had been fostered by historians. The significance of sociological theory for avant-garde activity thus exists in the manner in which it reflects orthodoxies about the past; indeed changes in the nature of sociological theorising, such as those which, as I shall indicate below, took place in Britain in the 1870s, generally parallel changes in historiography.

One of the intellectual conditions which determines the nature of sociological enquiry in a particular culture is the set of concepts about the past developed by historians. The other, more basic precondition is some initial doubt about the structure of society itself: only that doubt will provoke an enquiry into its nature in the first place. In France both these conditions were satisfied in a particularly dramatic way by the French Revolution and French revolutionary historiography. The tradition of analytical sociology developed there by August Comte was, in the first place, a reaction to the disruption and dislocation of revolution; it was an attempt to reconstruct society through the discovery of the basic principles of social order and the processes by which they gradually developed. The main objective of the sociologist was to explain social change through time; sociology, in other words, 'began, avowedly, as a historical science of society.'[21] Now although Comte's conception of a 'scientific' history was quite different from that of his fellow historians, nevertheless the manner in which he explained social change had many points of connection with the explanations of the French Revolution offered by historians such as Mignet, Thiers and Michelet: all shared a highly deterministic view of historical causation which virtually denied agency to individuals. For historians, as I have indicated, this view followed from a tendency to see the Revolution as an abstract force following a predetermined course. With Comte it was due to his positing a natural 'law' of social change – the three stages, theological, metaphysical and positivist, through which society passed – and his exclusive focus on a social entity which did not allow for any significant individual intervention in the historical process. (It is worth noting here that Comte was deeply contemptuous of all social reformers.) The development in nineteenth-century France of this particular tradition of social thought, with its vision of wholesale revolution and reconstruction, is ample testimony to the currency of the concepts of historical rupture and repudiation of tradition fundamental to avant-garde activity; Comte's new way of looking at society – his founding the new discipline called 'sociology' – can, in other words, be seen as a product of the same intellectual conditions which produced equally innovative ways of considering art and literature. Moreover, the hostile reaction to Comte's sociology by British intellectuals, and the very different kind of sociological enquiry which took place there, is in itself a good indication of the absence of those concepts in Britain.

Comte had many critics in Britain, the most vociferous being scientists (especially T. H. Huxley) and historians. Both these groups felt particularly defensive in the face of Comte's attempt to dispense with their disciplines and replace them with his new all-embracing 'scientific history'.[22] Two examples of this hostility, from the historians Charles Kingsley and Goldwin Smith, will indicate the general nature of British reactions to Comte. In his inaugural lecture as Professor of Modern History at Cambridge in 1860, Kingsley launched a scathing attack on the philosophies of history produced by French historians. Although Comte was not actually named, the disparaging reference to 'positivist sciences' and to its consequences made the target of his attack abundantly clear.

> Dazzled, and that pardonably, by the beauty of the few laws they may have discovered, they are too apt to erect them into gods, and to explain by them all matters in heaven and earth; and apt, too, . . . to patch them where they are weakest, by that most dangerous succedaneum of vague and grand epithets, which very often contain, each of them, an assumption far more important than the law to which they are tacked.[23]

Kingsley accepted Comte's general principles of 'order and progress' in history, but he argued that this did not imply the existence of quasi-scientific laws in history; history, he argued, properly belonged to the moral sciences, and hence whatever laws there might be existed 'not in things, but in persons; in the actions of human beings.' Progress, in other words, came about through the actions of great individuals inspired by God. At Oxford, at virtually the same time, Goldwin Smith delivered a similar set of lectures, directed, however, more specifically at Comte. Smith first rebutted the general proposition that there could be an inductive science of history, arguing that such a science was 'built on the quicksand of free will', and that by ignoring the individual it ruled out the only possible evidence for testing its generalisations about human behaviour. He then went on to dismiss Comte's law of the three stages and to disparage as 'jargon' his concepts of 'social statics' and 'dynamics'. In his second lecture he provided the following summary of his view of Comtean sociology:

> Till the law of history is not only laid down but shown to agree with the facts, or till humanity has been successfully treated by scientific methods, I confess I shall continue to suspect that the new science of Man is merely a set of terms, such as 'development,' 'social statics,' 'social dynamics,' 'organization,' and, above all, 'law,' scientifically applied to a subject to which in truth they are only metaphorically applicable: I shall continue to believe that human actions, in history as in individual life and in society, may and do present moral connections of the most intimate and momentous kind, but not that necessary sequence of causation on which alone science can be based; I shall continue to believe that humanity advances by free effort, but that it is not developed according to invariable laws, such as, when discovered, would give birth to a new science.[24]

Kenneth Boch has described the critiques of Kingsley and Smith as 'disappointing' in that they failed to address the methodological issues which Comte's view of history raised, and that they thus also failed to engage in a fruitful debate about the nature of historical causation and explanation.[25] This is only partly true. Kingsley and Smith, as historians, and thus holding, as I have indicated, very decided views on the nature of historiography, simply asserted that Comte's sociology was not history, and could therefore make no valid claim to have understood the past in a new way. Their reaction, then, was similar in nature to the rejection of Mignet's and Thiers' interpretation of the Revolution on the grounds that it was also 'bad' historiography. (Indeed it is significant that Kingsley understood Comte's sociology as a kind of history: it was another of those 'philosophies of history fostered by the French'.) Comte's analytical sociology never took hold in Britain: it failed as a scientific *history* to make any impression on the majority of British historians; but it also failed as an *analysis of society* to impress British sociologists who, proceeding from the premisses of Whiggish gradualism, had a fundamentally different conception of social enquiry.[26]

The main concern of British sociology was not with social change and reconstruction, nor was it with theorising about social structures and functions. Rather, and more prosaically, it sought to achieve ameliorative reform through governmental apparatuses in the belief that society was basically in good order and only needed superficial and piecemeal changes. The discipline was based on statistics, and policy was orientated towards improving conditions for the individual. Specifically, British sociologists spent most of their energies debating such topics as prison reform, sexual conduct, educational provisions, public health and so on, while at the same time proclaiming their hostility to 'all systems of opinion or doctrine'. For the first three-quarters of the century, then, British sociology was little more than institutionalised philanthropy.[27]

There were several reasons for the development of sociology in this direction in Britain. For example, as Philip Abrams has noted, institutional, financial and political factors played an important role. In the first place, the British intelligentsia, aligned with the country's social, political and ecclesiastical élites, found solutions to 'social problems' in a way which actively discouraged analytical sociology. Second, the universities and other institutions were also closed to sociologists. Without institutional support, sociologists needed to be very wealthy to fund the large-scale enquiries necessary for independent social analyses, and such projects rapidly became the property of Royal Commissions. Social theorists thus tended to become identified with the machinery of government. Moreover, as Abrams has also pointed out, political economy, with its emphasis on the individual and its popular association with *laissez-faire* economics, became the organising frame of reference for sociologists. It is clear, then, that the basic assumptions of British sociologists were virtually identical with those of British historians. They included a belief in gradual changes which did not involve major reconstructions of the social order; an emphasis on the individual as the only significant unit of social analysis; and a complacent faith in the essential soundness of the underlying structure and institutions of British society. British sociology reflected and perpetuated intellectual orthodoxies concerning the past and its relevance to the present: it confirmed, that is, the pervasiveness and authority of Whiggish gradualism.

The tendency of British intellectuals to treat French pro-revolutionary historiography and Comtean sociology as if they were identical was in fact part of a more widespread custom of attributing all foreign intellectual practices to the same root cause: revolutionary ideology. This became commonplace in the second half of the century: the 1848 Revolution had confirmed the British in their prejudices against everything French. Abstract theorising or systematising, repudiation of tradition, and the denial of individual agency and individual moral responsibility were all seen to be evidence of that most extreme form of revolutionary thinking – Jacobinism. For many British intellectuals 'the ways of Jacobinism' became a portmanteau phrase for everything which threatened to subvert British cultural and intellectual traditions, including avant-garde art and literature. The characterisation of British avant-gardism as Jacobin is discussed in later chapters, but two examples will illustrate how pervasive the strategy was. They provide very clear evidence too for the existence of the intellectual connections between art and literature and other disciplines of knowledge. The first, worth quoting at length, is Matthew Arnold's discovery of traces of Jacobinism in British intellectual life and his indictment of its evils in *Culture and Anarchy*:

> I may call them the ways of Jacobinism. Violent indignation with the past, abstract systems of renovation applied wholesale, a new doctrine drawn up in black and white for elaborating . . . a rational society for the future, – these are the ways of Jacobinism. . . . Culture is the eternal opponent of the two things which are signal marks of Jacobinism, – its fierceness, and its addiction to an abstract system. . . . Culture tends always thus to deal with the men of a system, of disciples, of a school; with men like Comte or, the late Mr. Buckle, or Mr. Mill. However much it may find to admire in these personages, or in some of them, it nevertheless remembers the text: 'Be not ye called Rabbi!' . . . But Jacobinism loves a Rabbi . . . [;] it wants its Rabbi and his ideas to stand for perfection, that they may with the more authority recast the world; and for Jacobinism, therefore, culture . . . is an impertinence and an offence. . . . So, too, Jacobinism, in its fierce hatred of the past and of those whom it makes liable for the sins of the past, cannot away with the inexhaustible indulgence proper to culture, the consideration of circumstances, the severe judgement of actions joined to the merciful judgement of persons.[28]

The second example is an article in the *National Review* by William Courthope which discussed 'Conservatism in Art'.[29] Courthope begins by making the familiar classical comparison between 'the constitution of a genuine work of art' and 'that of a well ordered state'. However, he goes on to draw attention to the similarity between 'an artistic Radicalism asserting the claims of abstract theory against those of authority and tradition' and 'Jacobinism': both, he argued, refused 'to be bound by law', and both 'insist that genius is . . . to be judged by certain laws of its own intelligible only to the initiated.' There then follows a description of Swinburne's review of Rossetti in terms derived directly from the French Revolution: it was 'critical terrorism'. (Interestingly this term was not new; two years earlier, another hostile critic of Swinburne, the French scholar Arthur Tilley, had described 'Swinburne's ideal poet' as 'an impassioned rhapsodist . . . pouring forth wild musical words in praise of the eternal truths of liberty, fraternity, and equality.')[30] Courthope closed his discussion with the demand that all art be submitted to 'Authority', be brought 'before the court of those great masters in . . . art whose position has been established by the consent of ages.' He claimed not to be against artistic innovation itself, and argued that due consideration be given to 'the liberty of the individual', and to 'social changes of thought, feeling, prejudice, and custom, and . . . the desire of novelty which is undoubtedly an instinct in the human mind, when judging the "modern".' Nevertheless he insisted that the innovative artist be judged by 'Conservative' principles; by 'veneration [for] . . . the continuous tradition and authority of "the national past out of which he proceeded".'

The different dates of these two accounts are significant. Arnold, writing in 1869, warned of an impending danger; the 'ways of Jacobinism' were as yet 'novel and untried' in Britain. However, by contrast, in 1883, Courthope describes events which had already taken place in Britain. What then had happened in the intervening years to bring about this change? How did the 'ways of Jacobinism', intellectually alien to Britain for the first three-quarters of the century, eventually find their way there? Or, to put these questions in the specific context of avant-gardism, how, and why, did the avant-garde which Courthope identifies develop in Britain in the last quarter of the century? What changes had there been in the intellectual climate to make conditions more amenable to the development of an avant-garde at this particular moment? In fact what had occurred in the 1870s was a crisis of intellectual authority which was felt in most disciplines of knowledge – in political economy, sociology, historiography, psychology, aesthetics, mathematics and so on.[31] Its immediate effect was to throw doubt on the orthodoxies which had dominated the intellectual climate for the first three-quarters of the century. This in turn allowed, for a brief and liberating moment, the contemplation of 'foreign' ideas. One product of this new sense of intellectual freedom was British avant-gardism; others included Spencerian sociology and Jevonian economics.

The causes of this crisis are too various and complex to discuss in detail here. Briefly, though, they include the following factors: the social and political upheavals of the 1860s, and the economic malaise of the late 1870s and early 1880s, which together made it increasingly difficult to sustain the view that the structure of society and social institutions were fundamentally sound. As a consequence, many of the assumptions which had proceeded from these beliefs – the Whiggish assumption that progress was gradual and continuous, and the ameliorist assumption that radical reconstructions of social theory were unnecessary – became increasingly untenable. A further consequence was the loss of authority of the historical and sociological explanations which these assumptions had underwritten.[32] Important too were the new and contemporaneous pressures being exerted by the twin processes of specialisation and professionalisation. As knowledge increased during the century so it became divided into discrete fields, each of which demanded its own experts. This led to the authority of the Victorian 'sage' – Mill or Carlyle, for example – gradually being replaced by that of the specialist, with the consequence that the generalist explanations characteristic of disciplines such as historiography and political economy earlier in the century tended to lose their prestige.[33] Of related importance were the effects of the explosive growth in science and technology in the latter half of the century. All disciplines came under pressure to become more rigorous by adopting methodologies similar to those of the natural sciences, and to be 'scientific' became virtually synonymous with being authoritative.[34] Finally, there were also important changes in epistemology in the last quarter of the century, the appearance of new and competing models of man led to conflicts of authority between the explanations they underwrote.[35]

The details of all these contributory factors have been documented elsewhere and need not be repeated here since my main concern is with the effects of this crisis on the authority of those two disciplines, historiography and sociology, which have most influence in shaping a culture's perception of the past. Initially, however, as I suggested earlier in Chapter 2, it is important for two reasons to glance briefly at the crisis of authority in political economy. In the first place, there is its 'exemplary' nature – the effects of the crisis are most visible and dramatic in political economy and they give a fair indication of the profound nature of the intellectual disquiet which the crisis produced. Second, there is the unique status of political economy in nineteenth-century Britain: the hegemony of its all-embracing explanations – it claimed to account for all aspects of life, not just the economic – effectively made political economy the dominant ideology and clearly a crisis in its authority would have contributed to the doubts felt in the explanations of other disciplines of knowledge – particularly historiography and sociology which shared its assumptions.[36]

Political economy had had its critics throughout the nineteenth century, but its authority was never seriously threatened until the late 1860s when it came under attack from a number of quarters. First from John Stuart Mill, who disputed two of its major tenets in 1869; and then subsequently from the theory of marginal utility developed in Britain by William Stanley Jevons, and the critique mounted by Cliffe Leslie and William Cunningham of the 'historical school'.[37] The consequence of these combined assaults was the eventual transformation of classical political economy into the specialised discipline of economics which is familiar today. The actual nature of this transformation is a much debated issue,[38] but what is not in doubt is that the authority of political economy dwindled dramatically in the 1870s, precipitating 'a period of heart searching and stocktaking in economic thought.'[39] Although by the end of the decade it was abundantly clear that there was a need for some dramatic reconstruction in economic thinking, the dominant school to emerge from the crisis was in many respects a conservative return to pre-Jevonian thinking. The task of reforming economics largely fell to Alfred Marshall, professor of political economy in Cambridge in 1885. Marshall, who has been described as 'an intellectual coward',[40] was conspicuous in his attempt to play down Jevons's challenge (particularly in value theory) by reviving some 'classical' concepts and terms. His reasons for so doing are highly significant: '_continuity of tradition_', Marshall argued, '_is important everywhere_; it is nowhere more important than in our use of terms; while in our use of terms it is even more important as regards the _tone_ or _flavour_ which they connote, than as regards the boundaries marked out by their formal definitions.'[41] The process by which political economy was eventually replaced by marginal utility theory was thus slow, held up for a time by the dominance of the counter-revolutionary Marshallian school. The reasons for this situation are complex – personal, intellectual, social and institutional reasons all played a part.[42] The significant point, however, is that the slow response to Jevons's radical theoretical critique was not untypical. In fact a similar pattern, that of theoretical innovation in the 1870s followed by partial revisionism in the 1880s, characterises the developments at this time in many other disciplines of knowledge. This process in turn suggests that many of the conservative orthodoxies which had dominated the intellectual climate for the first three-quarters of the century did in fact survive the brief hiatus of the 1870s and continued in the 1880s, albeit in a weaker form and exerting a weaker pressure, to circumscribe intellectual activity.

One such case occurred in the status of sociology. By the early 1870s, the collapse of political economy, the economic malaise, and the social and political upheavals of the late 1860s had all combined to undermine the confidence of ameliorist sociology. For the first time conditions pointed to the need for a major reconstruction of society – for sociological theorising rather than simply piecemeal social changes – and this new need coincided with the appearance of a new historical sociology and a flowering of social theory. For the first time in Britain, in the work of Herbert Spencer, sociology addressed itself to the problem of social change and the resultant evolutionary sociology marked as radical a departure from the orthodoxies of statisticians and ameliorists as Jevons's marginal utility theory had from classical political economy. Spencer's massive *Principles of Sociology* was published over a number of years from 1876 to 1896, but in 1873 he brought out the more polemical *The Study of Sociology*, a kind of prolegomenon to the *Principles* which rehearsed the issues and problems which he saw as central to sociological enquiry.[43] Spencer began by discussing the fundamental question of whether sociology was comparable to the natural sciences; whether, that is, it could discover regularities in human behaviour which were amenable to natural laws:

If there is no natural causation throughout the actions of incorporated humanity, government and legislation are absurd. Acts of Parliament may, as well as not, be made to depend on the drawing of lots or the tossing of a coin; or, rather, there may as well be none at all: social sequences having no ascertainable order, no effect can be counted on

– everything is chaotic. On the other hand, if there is natural causation, then the combination of forces by which every combination of effects is produced, produces that combination of effects in conformity with the laws of the forces. And if so, it behoves us to use all diligence in ascertaining what the forces are, what are their laws, and what are the ways in which they co-operate.[44]

Having established that such laws had logically to exist, Spencer then argued that they were in fact to be found in the pattern of differentiation exhibited in the basic processes underlying the elaboration of social structure. Social change was thus explained in terms of an organism – society – with functionally interdependent parts which evolved through structural differentiation. Such a view was highly deterministic; in a manner similar to, but by no means identical with Comtean sociology, this view appeared to deny that individuals could influence social change – the only function sociology had was to impress upon men the futility of their efforts to improve social conditions through legislative reform. Such an automatic and mechanistic concept of evolution was anathema not only to ameliorists but also to historians, because Spencer, once more like Comte, seemed to have disregarded totally the importance of individual human agency. Indeed in *The Study of Sociology* Spencer presented a detailed and thorough critique of the kind of explanations hitherto offered by British historians. He argued that because they used material such as 'the doings of kings, court-intrigues, international quarrels, victories and defeats . . . all of which have no definite forecast', historians were reduced to seeking causal explanations either in terms of the motives of great men or the intercession of providence; and such explanations were invalid because profoundly unscientific.[45] Indeed the only role Spencer saw for historians was to furnish sociologists with the raw materials which the latter group would then subsequently explain. In the context of the sociological and historiographical orthodoxies outlined above, Spencer's intellectual achievement was, as Philip Abrams has suggested, little short of 'astounding'. However, such an achievement was only conceivable in a climate where the orthodoxies which it had reacted against had already been severely undermined. Spencer's highly deterministic, evolutionary sociology was thus testimony to the profound intellectual hiatus in the 1870s already noted. Moreover, both the subsequent adverse reaction to his work, and the consequent failure of any tradition of theoretical sociology to establish itself in Britain, are testimony to the resurgence in the 1880s of an intellectual conservatism. Spencer's theories, though sufficiently remarkable to initiate a debate about the future direction of sociological enquiry, were too controversial, too 'alien' to British intellectual traditions, to have much positive influence on its outcome. As Abrams has suggested, British sociology was rebuilt in the 1880s and 1890s as a defence against Spencer. Indeed, significantly the only figure after Spencer to argue for the importance of sociological theory, Leonard Trelawney Hobhouse, differed from him in nearly every respect except a general emphasis on evolution-ary principles. Hobhouse contrived a new sociology, based on the biological evolution of the mind, which did not require society to progress in any particular direction, and which advocated bene-volent social intervention. But even this programme found few advocates, and, already marginalised, theoretical sociology quickly became the object of derision – its practitioners branded as 'rich visionaries, academic eccentrics . . . and social biologists'.[46] A tradition of theroetical sociology in Britain did not finally establish itself – and even then not particularly successfully – until the second half of the present century.

Another such intellectual crisis occurred in British historiography. This crisis may appear less dramatic than that in sociology and political economy in so far as it was a crisis in scholarship and methodology rather than theory – there was, for example, no historian of a standing to equal the prestige of Jevons or Spencer. (Henry Thomas Buckle, who is discussed below, did not have the same kind of intellectual prestige as these other figures.) However, the crisis in historiography is still significant in that it demonstrates the extent to which the authority of a whole body of historical writing – a whole tradition of historiography – was radically called into question. One important consequence was that the views of the past which that work had been instrumental in establishing in terms of an orthodoxy, suddenly became, in the 1870s, much less convincing.

The first main challenge to the authority of historians such as Mackintosh and Macaulay in fact came in the late 1850s from Henry Thomas Buckle's *History of Civilization in England* (1857–61).[47] In a manner similar to French sociologists (to whom he was indebted), Buckle argued that historical enquiry should have as its ambition the establishing of universal laws. Such an ambition was possible,

Buckle suggested, because human social behaviour exhibited the same regularity as natural phenomena; history could (and should) take as its model the natural sciences. The result of these premises was a positivist history which made Buckle a great celebrity with the reading public but which brought him little success with the intellectual establishment. The reasons were partly personal: Buckle, proud of his auto-didacticism, never lost the opportunity of voicing his contempt for the standards of Oxford and Cambridge.[48] But there were other, intellectual reasons: his deterministic model of man – his view of the moral disposition as fixed – and his materialist laws of causation ran counter to the traditional emphasis in British historiography on free will and moral agency described above.[49] Buckle's *History*, though widely reviewed by figures as eminent as Lord Acton, Leslie Stephen and Sir Henry Maine,[50] was never considered seriously as a proposal for the reform of historical research; in a manner similar to the treatment of Comte, Buckle's work was simply dismissed as 'bad' historiography, and he remained a marginal figure in intellectual circles. Nevertheless Buckle *is* a significant figure if only in the sense that, like many French historians of the Revolution, he influenced the development of historical scholarship negatively. When in the following decade other pressures forced historians to review their practices, the model of historiography which they chose was deliberately not that suggested by Buckle.

It was not until the late 1860s, under the growing pressures from the general processes of professionalisation and specialisation, that the old conceptions of a historian as gentleman rather than scholar, and of history as 'a compound of poetry and philosophy',[51] finally became both untenable and unworkable.[52] By this time it was clear that historiography, as Buckle had predicted, was indeed in need of radical reform if its authority in the newly specialised, 'scientific' world was not to be placed in jeopardy. However, the most suitable model for reformers to adopt was neither that of Buckle nor of Comte, but rather that of the new methodologies being developed in Germany – particularly by the Rankean school. Ranke's emphasis upon 'facts', upon the importance of archival evidence and the critical examination of sources, gave a new and much needed rigour to historical scholarship which made a valid claim for historiography to be *Wissenschaft*. In Britain, Rankean history found its most enthusiastic supporter in William Stubbs, Regius Professor of

Modern History at Oxford from 1866 to 1884. In his inaugural lecture in 1867, Stubbs spoke admiringly of 'the great German hive of historical scholars' and described his own role in:

> founding . . . an historical school in England, which shall join with the other workers of Europe in a common task; which shall build, not upon Hallam and Palgrave and Kemble and Froude and Macaulay, but on the abundant collected and arranged materials on which those writers tried to build whilst they were scanty and scattered and in disorder.[53]

Although initially there was some hostility to Ranke, particularly to the idealist temper of his thought, Stubbs's new school was nevertheless remarkably successful, and in historians such as T. F. Tout and J. R. Round he found willing and able followers.

Now there are several general points to be made about attitudes towards the past exhibited in this crisis in historiography. In the first place it is clear that the work of early historians such as Macaulay and Mackintosh, which had been so instrumental in creating the orthodoxies about the past which worked against the development of avant-gardism in Britain, had been largely discredited as unsophisticated and impressionistic by the early 1870s. Moreover, at a general level, the authority of all historians had been called into question; as the appearance of Spencer's evolutionary sociology demonstrated, historians could no longer confidently claim to have a monopoly on an ability to interpret the past. Against this circumstance has to be placed the fact that the move towards a more 'scientific' history which took place in historiography in the 1880s followed the conservative German example rather than the path suggested by Buckle. German historiography was attractive not only because of its scholarly rigour, but also because of its 'democratic and populist account of constitutional origins'; the idea of 'the creation of the constitution . . . by a long, spontaneous, almost imperceptible process of consolidation and registration of custom'[54] was easily assimilated into traditions of British Whiggism. The appropriation of German scholarship did not, that is, involve any major reassessment of traditional British philosophies of history. Despite a period of uncertainty over its methods and direction in the 1870s, when British historiography did finally reform itself, it retained the emphasis on tradition and continuity with the past. Such a process, the importance of which is described below, explains why the avant-garde which emerged in Britain in the last quarter of the nineteenth century was intent on reinterpreting the past while at the same time retaining a profound respect for tradition.

The objective in this chapter has been to determine the intellectual conditions for avant-garde activity in nineteenth-century Britain, and from these conditions several conclusions may be drawn. First, it is clear that for the first seventy years of the century the intellectual climate in Britain was profoundly hostile to the development of the kind of avant-garde activity which took place in France. The revolutionary concepts of historical rupture and of repudiation of the authority of tradition which were necessary to such a development – these were simply alien to British culture. The only significant challenge to artistic orthodoxies to appear during this period was the formation of the Pre-Raphaelite Brotherhood in the late 1840s. I shall discuss this movement in more detail in a later chapter in relation to the political and aesthetic theories of William Morris. For the moment, however, it is sufficient to point out that the Pre-Raphaelites, although opposed to the teaching of the Academy, and although claiming to address a popular audience, had a quite different artistic programme from artists such as Courbet. Far from rejecting tradition, the Pre-Raphaelite Brotherhood emulated fifteenth-century Italian paintings with the declared aim of *restoring* an authentic tradition of Western art. Theirs was no more and no less than a 'Glorious Revolution' in painting. The second point to notice is that these intellectual conditions changed dramatically in the 1870s with the crisis of authority in Britain at this time. I have attempted, at a general level, to indicate the depth of this crisis; more specifically I have highlighted its effects on those disciplines most influential in shaping a culture's attitudes towards the past, suggesting that the lack of confidence in traditional historiography coincided with the advent of the first sustained theory of social change. It was during this period of general intellectual disquiet and of specific changes in attitudes towards the past that conditions in Britain came closest to (although they were still distant from) those which had allowed in France the development of an avant-garde consciousness intent on totally repudiating the past. The attempts by figures such as Pater and Swinburne to subvert literary and artistic orthodoxies in the 1870s thus mark the first emergence in Britain of a literary avant-garde equally provocative and subversive, although for different reasons and in different ways, as those which had developed earlier in France. Despite this, as I have also noted, many conservative orthodoxies survived the hiatus of the 1870s and returned, albeit in a weaker form, to circumscribe intellectual activities, including those of the nascent British avant-garde. The strategies of opposition to the past adopted by writers such as Pater, Wilde and Morris in the 1880s and 1890s have to be assessed in the context of these continuing intellectual constraints.

By way of a preface to my discussion of this intellectual context, I cited two familiar examples of French avant-garde artists, Manet and Courbet, both of whom exhibited a disrespect for the past and a self-confidence in their own authority as 'moderns' to act independently of traditional models of authority; and I suggested that these activities could be explained in terms of the revolutionary concepts then readily available to them. In Britain, where the dominant attitude towards the past remained that of historical continuity and a profound reverence for tradition, avant-garde activity was quite different. Whatever their aesthetic or political theories, *all* British avant-garde writers in the nineteenth century had to accommodate *themselves* to a tradition, not a tradition to their work. Indeed all consistently invoked the authority of past writers to validate their own practices. However, as I shall argue, this fact did not necessarily mean that their artistic programmes were any less subversive than those of their French contemporaries. While they did not totally disregard tradition (as Courbet did), and while they did not ever deny (in the way Manet seemed to) that a tradition could have authority and relevance for the present, the use of tradition made by these writers was nevertheless quite different to that of their contemporaries. In the case of the avant-gardism of, say, Swinburne and Pater, who were intent on redefining the nature and function of art and literature, the necessity of accommodating themselves to tradition involved appropriating and redefining the work of some past writers in a way which authorised their own avant-garde practices. It involved, that is, creating, in Pater's words, a 'constant tradition' of Aestheticism – a process which profoundly undermined the moral and social functions which were then usually ascribed to a literary tradition. What appears in these writers to be profoundly conservative on closer inspection turns out to be politically subversive.

Notes

1. See for example R. K. R. Thornton, *The Decadent Dilemma* (London: Edward Arnold, 1983); Ruth Z. Temple, 'Truth in labelling: Pre-Raphaelitism, Aestheticism, Decadence, Fin de Siècle', *English Literature in Transition*, 17 (1974), 201–22; James K. Robinson, 'A neglected phase of the aesthetic movement: English parnassianism', *PMLA*, 68 (1953), 733–54.

2. The only factor cited as inhibiting the transfer of ideas between the two countries, and thus accounting for the apparent timidity of British avant-gardes, is the more restrictive censorship laws which operated in Britain in the late nineteenth century. (See Thornton, op. cit., for example.) However the relationship between avant-garde polemic and censorship is a vexed one, as an equally convincing case can be made to support the opposite view: i.e. that the most radical avant-garde polemic is produced in the most restrictive societies. See for example, Donald Drew Egbert, 'The idea of the "avant-garde" in art and politics', *American Historical Review*, 73 (1967), 339–66.

3. See Ian Small, 'The French Revolution and British Culture' in Ceri Crossley and Ian Small (eds.), *The French Revolution and British Culture* (Oxford: Oxford University Press, 1989), ix–xviii.

4. See Geoffrey Hawthorn, *Enlightenment and Despair: A history of social theory* (2nd edn, Cambridge: Cambridge University Press, 1987).

5. François Mignet, *Histoire de la Révolution Française* (16th edn, Paris, 1887), I, 2.

6. See, for example, Linda Nochlin, *Gustave Courbet: A study in style and society* (New York: Garland, 1976); and T. J. Clark, *Image of the People: Gustave Courbet and the 1848 Revolution* (London: Thames and Hudson, 1973).

7. See Nochlin, op. cit.; Meyer Schapiro, 'Courbet and Popular Imagery: An essay on Realism and Naiveté', *Journal of the Warburg and Courtauld Institute*, 4 (1940–1), 164–91; and Joseph Sloane, *French Painting between the Past and the Present* (Princeton, N.J.: Princeton University Press, 1951).

8. Sloane, 80.

9. There is some debate over whether or not Manet 'intended' these paintings to be provocative. Joseph Sloane argues that although Manet was self-consciously 'modern', he did not set out to shock his public, nor did he think of his art either as immoral or as a challenge to an artistic tradition; indeed he was genuinely 'astonished' at the adverse reaction of his critics (see Sloane, 181–4). In contrast to this view, Linda Nochlin argues that Manet is not to be taken at his word when he expresses surprise at the hostile reaction of his critics, and that his works are 'monumental and ironic put-ons, *blagues*.' (See Nochlin, 'The invention of the avant-garde' in Thomas B. Hess and John Ashbery,

(eds.), *The Avant-Garde, Art News Annual*, 34 (1968), 16.) A middle course is steered by Theodore Reff in *Manet: Olympia* (London: Allen Lane, 1976). Reff, although disagreeing with Nochlin, argues that, whatever his intentions might have been, Manet's 'deliberate allusions to older art . . . is one of the reasons that his art of the period seems modern' and that at the very least, his 'gesture seemed ambiguous and disturbing' (59–60). I agree with Reff in that what is interesting is not Manet's 'intention' but rather the reasons why he felt enabled to 'use' tradition in this way.

10. Georges Seurat, for example, had an ambiguous attitude towards tradition. An almost obsessive desire to be original was accompanied by an apparent respect for tradition – hence his desire to be 'the Giotto of the age of Science'. (See François Cachin, 'The neo-impressionist avant-garde' in Hess and Ashbery (eds.), *The Avant-Garde*, 55–64.)

11. For an account of the 'liberal' interpretation and its dominance over the 'conservative' view, see Stanley Mellon, *The Political Uses of History: A study of historians in the Restoration* (Stanford: Stanford University Press, 1958).

12. Roger Scruton, 'Man's second disobedience: A vindication of Burke' in Ceri Crossley and Ian Small (eds.), *The French Revolution and British Culture*, 197 and 215.

13. Mignet, 4–5.

14. Jules Michelet, *Histoire de la Révolution Française* (Revised edn, Paris, 1869), I, vii–viii.

15. Although in saying this, I recognise that a precise account of the strategies of opposition to the past developed by particular avant-gardes would have to take account of all the many changes in the social, political and intellectual climate throughout the century which made this interpretation at times seem more or less plausible, and more or less authoritative.

16. See Hedva Ben-Israel, *Historians on the French Revolution* (Cambridge: Cambridge University Press, 1968). See also the relevant chapters in G. P. Gooch, *History and Historians in the Nineteenth Century* (2nd edn, London: Longman, 1952); and in Ernst Breisach, *Historiography: Ancient, medieval and modern* (London: University of Chicago Press, 1983); and Joseph Hamburger's Introduction to his edition of Macaulay's unfinished 'History of France', Thomas Babington Macaulay, *Napoleon and the Restoration of the Bourbons*, ed. Joseph Hamburger (London: Longman, 1977). The developments in British historiography in the nineteenth century have been amply documented. However, few accounts have related these developments to wider changes in British intellectual life, and virtually none have used them to explain changes in literary and artistic culture.

17. See J. W. Burrow, *A Liberal Descent: Victorians and the English past* (Cambridge: Cambridge University Press, 1981).

18. T. B. Macaulay, 'Dumont's *Recollections of Mirabeau* – The French Revolution', *Edinburgh Review*, 55 (1832), 572.

19. Macaulay, *The History of England* in Lady Trevelyan (ed.), *The Works of*

Lord Macaulay (London: Longman, 1897), II, 395–6. Quoted in Burrow, 48.

20. Sir James Mackintosh, *History of the Revolution in England in 1688* (London: Longman, 1834), 302. For a recent account of some of the ways in which the French Revolution changed the meaning of the term 'revolution' in Britain see George Woodcock, 'The meaning of revolution in Britain: 1770–1800' in Ceri Crossley and Ian Small (eds.), *The French Revolution and British Culture*, 1–30.

21. Kenneth Boch, *The Acceptance of Histories: Towards a perspective for social science, University of California Publications in Sociology and Social Institutions* (Berkeley and Los Angeles: University of California Press, 1956), 16.

22. The only sustained support for Comte came from outside the intellectual establishment, from what T. R. Wright refers to as 'the lunatic fringe of Victorian thinking'. A rather fragmented group, confining their energies to setting up a 'Church of Humanity' which itself underwent at least one major schism and several minor ones, they were generally 'tolerated' as harmless, because marginal eccentrics. See T. R. Wright, *The Religion of Humanity* (Cambridge: Cambridge University Press, 1986). For an opposing interpretation of the marginalisation of Comtism in Britain see Christopher Kent, *Brains and Numbers: Elitism, Comtism and democracy in mid-Victorian Britain* (London: University of Toronto Press, 1978). Kent argues that Comtism appealed to middle-class amateurism, and that in view of this circumstance what is remarkable about Comte is his lack of popularity in Britain. See also T. W. Heyck, *The Transformation of Intellectual Life in Victorian England* (London: Croom Helm, 1982).

23. Charles Kingsley, *The Limits of Exact Science as Applied to History*, (Cambridge: J.H. Parker and Son, 1860), 17.

24. Goldwin Smith, *Lectures on Modern History Delivered at Oxford 1859–61* (Oxford: J. H. Parker and Son, 1861), Lecture II, 45–6.

25. Boch, 33.

26. When referring to British social thought in the first seventy years of the nineteenth century, I use the terms 'sociology' and 'sociologists' for the sake of convenience rather than accuracy. In the usual understanding of the terms, sociological thinking implies some major theoretical enquiry into social structures. For this reason the first sociologist proper in Britain is generally held to be Herbert Spencer.

27. For the development of social thought in Britain see Philip Abrams, *The Origins of British Sociology* (London: University of Chicago Press, 1968); Geoffrey Hawthorn, op. cit; J. W. Burrow, *Evolution and Society: A study in Victorian social theory* (London: Cambridge University Press, 1966); Jerzy Szacki, *History of Sociological Thought* (London: Aldwych Press, 1979); and Maurice Mandelbaum, *History, Man and Reason: A study in nineteenth century thought* (London: Johns Hopkins Press, 1971).

28. Matthew Arnold, *Culture and Anarchy*, ed. J. Dover Wilson (Cambridge: Cambridge University Press, 1984), 65–8.

29. William J. Courthope, 'Conservatism in art', *National Review*, 1 (1883a), 72–84.

30. Arthur Tilley, 'Two Theories of Poetry', *Macmillan's Magazine*, 44 (1881), 271.

31. The significance of this general intellectual crisis for developments in literary culture has also been noted by Ian Small. However, he has seen it as an explanation of a different set of changes, those which took place in the writing of literary criticism in the 1870s and 1880s. See Ian Small, *Conditions for Criticism: Authority, knowledge, and literature in the late nineteenth century* (Oxford: Clarendon Press, 1991).

32. Burrow, for example, has emphasised the role played by the 1867 call for a widening of the suffrage in denting confidence in Whiggish gradualism. He argues that it suggested impending radical – rather than gradual – changes: 'the security for the progressive Whig,' Burrows points out, 'lies in the belief that modernity is essentially homogeneous and therefore exacts no agonising choices.' When this modernity was exposed as problematic, as it was by agitation for reform, then the complacency of Whiggism was severely undermined. See Burrow, 103.

33. For a general discussion of the processes of professionalisation see: *Daedalus*, 92 (Fall, 1963), a number which is devoted entirely to the professions; M. S. Larson, *The Rise of Professionalism: a sociological analysis* (London: University of California Press, 1977); Geoffrey Millerson, *The Qualifying Associations: A study in professionalization* (London: Routledge and Kegan Paul, 1964); A. H. Halsey and M. A. Trow, *The British Academics* (London: Faber and Faber, 1971) and J. A. Jackson (ed.), *Professions and Professionalization* (London: Cambridge University Press, 1970). For an account of professionalisation in nineteenth-century Britain see W. J. Reader, *Professional Men: The rise of the professional classes in nineteenth-century Britain* (London: Weidenfeld and Nicolson, 1966). For the specific effects of these processes within universities see T. W. Heyck, 'The idea of a university in Britain, 1870–1970', *History of European Ideas*, 8 (1987), 205–19; Sheldon Rothblatt, *The Revolution of the Dons* (London: Faber and Faber, 1968); Anthony Kearney, *John Churton Collins: The louse on the locks of literature* (Edinburgh: Scottish Academic Press, 1986); and Christopher Harvie, *The Lights of Liberalism* (London: Allen Lane, 1976). Finally, for the effects of these processes on writers see Robert L. Patten, '"The people have set literature free": The professionalization of letters in nineteenth-century England', *Review*, 9 (1987),

34. See for example, T. W. Heyck, *The Transformation of Intellectual Life in Victorian England* (London: Croom Helm, 1982).

35. See Kenneth Boch, op. cit.; Clifford Geertz, *The Interpretation of Cultures* (New York: Basic Books, 1973); Ian Small, *Conditions for Criticism*, op. cit.

36. The question of whether the collapse of political economy was catalyst or symptom of the intellectual crisis is a vexed one.

37. For a discussion of the collapse of political economy see the edition of

The Manchester School, 2 (May, 1951) marking the centenary of Jevons's death; the relevant chapters in Robert B. Ekelund Jr and Robert F. Hébert, *A History of Economic Thinking* (London: McGraw Hill, 1975); Robert M. Fisher, *The Logic of Economic Discovery: Neoclassical economics and the marginalist revolution* (Brighton: Wheatsheaf, 1986); T. W. Hutchison, *A Review of Economic Doctrines 1870–1929* (Westport, Conn.: Greenwood Press, 1975) and *On Revolutions and Progress in Economic Knowledge* (Cambridge: Cambridge University Press, 1978); R. D. Collison Black, 'W. S. Jevons and the Foundation of Modern Economics', *History of Political Economy*, 4 (1972), 365–78; Paul Adelman, 'Frederick Harrison and the "positivist" attack on orthodox political economy', *History of Political Economy*, 3 (1971), 170–89; Gerald M. Koot, 'English historical economics and the emergence of economic history in England', *History of Political Economy*, 12 (1980), 174–205; Lawrence Birken, 'From macroeconomic to microeconomics: the marginalist revolution in sociocultural perspective', *History of Political Economy*, 20 (1988), 251–64.

38. This debate is documented in R. D. Collison Black, A. W. Coats, Crawfurd D. W. Goodwin (eds.), *The Marginalist Revolution in Economics: Interpretation and evaluation* (Durham, N. Carolina: Duke University Press, 1973).

39. Collison Black, 'W. S. Jevons and the Foundation of Modern Economics', 376.

40. A. W. Coats, 'Sociological aspects of British economic thought (CA 1880–1930)', *Journal of Political Economy*, 75 (1967), 710.

41. Alfred Marshall, 'Distribution and exchange', *Economic Journal*, 8 (1898), 57. (My emphasis.)

42. See Coats, 'Sociological aspects of British economic thought (CA 1880–1930)'.

43. Herbert Spencer, *Principles of Sociology*, 3 vols. (London: Williams and Norgate, 1876–96); *The Study of Sociology* (London: Kegan, Paul and Trench, 1873). The latter was also published simultaneously in periodical instalments – in Britain in the *Contemporary Review*, and in the United States in *Popular Science Monthly*.

44. Spencer, *The Study of Sociology* (13th edn, London: Henry S. King, 1887), 46–7.

45. For Spencer's critique of contemporary historiography see *The Study of Sociology* (1887), 25–44.

46. Hawthorn, 111.

47. Henry Thomas Buckle, *History of Civilization in England*, 2 vols. (London: J. W. Parker and Son, 1857–61).

48. See Giles St Aubyn, *A Victorian Eminence* (London: Barrie Books, 1958), 5, 180–1.

49. See T. W. Heyck, *The Transformation of Intellectual Life in Victorian England*, 133–40.

50. See John Mackinnon Robertson, *Buckle and his Critics: A study in sociology* (London: Swan Sonnenschein and Co., 1895).

51. Macaulay, 'Hallam's constitutional history', *Edinburgh Review*, 48 (1828), 96.
52. For the professionalisation of British history see Phillipa Levine, *The Amateur and the Professional: Antiquarians, historians and archaeologists in Victorian England, 1838–1886* (Cambridge: Cambridge University Press, 1986); Doris Goldstein, 'The professionalization of history in Britain in the late nineteenth and early twentieth centuries', *Storia Della Storiografia*, 1 (1983), 3–27 and 'The organizational development of the British historical profession, 1884–1921', *Bulletin of the Institute of Historical Research*, 55 (1982), 180–93; Llewllyn Woodward, 'The rise of the professional historian' in K. Bourne and D. C. Watt (eds.), *Studies in International History* (London: Longman, 1987), 16–34; Rosemary Jann, 'From amateur to professional: The case of the Oxbridge historians', *Journal of British Studies*, 2 (1983), 122–47; A. T. Milne, 'History at the universities: then and now', *History*, 59 (1974), 33–46; Herbert Butterfield, 'Delays and paradoxes in the development of historiography' in K. Bourne and D. C. Watt (eds.), *Studies in International History* (London: Longman, 1987), 1–15 and 'Some trends in scholarship 1868–1968 in the field of modern history', *Transactions of the Royal Historical Society*, 5th series, 19 (1969), 159–84.
53. William Stubbs, *Seventeen Lectures on the Study of Medieval and Modern History and Kindred Subjects* (3rd edn, Oxford: Clarendon Press, 1900), 13–14.
54. Burrow, *A Liberal Descent*, 125 and 126.

PART II

Politics

CHAPTER 4

The politics of obscurity: Theorising tradition

The first signs that conditions for literary and artistic activities were changing in Britain, and that it was becoming possible for oppositional artists and writers to challenge the pervasive power of tradition, are to be found in the debates about obscurity in the 1870s and 1880s. In these debates assumptions about the unproblematic nature of the relationship between the writer and tradition were called into question, and the whole issue of literary and artistic innovation was brought into sharp focus. Obscurity, in other words, raised exactly those issues central to avant-garde activities. In this sense the debates about obscurity, although involving relatively minor publications, are an important source of evidence that the necessary preconditions for avant-garde activities had begun to develop in Britain.

During the first three-quarters of the nineteenth century, the term obscurity invariably constituted an adverse judgement on unorthodox or unusual styles of writing. It was used to describe peculiarities of syntax and vocabulary, or irregularities of metre and rhythm – indeed any textual feature which could be a source of alleged incomprehension. Obscurity was defined, then, in terms of a set of linguistic norms, and these norms were in their turn defined in terms of the requirements of a 'general' audience. The label 'obscure' thus functioned as a means of marginalising innovative or oppositional work because as a label it was used to deny to that work the title of 'literature'. In the late 1860s and early 1870s a small group of writers, chiefly Algernon Swinburne, Dante Gabriel Rossetti and Walter Pater, contested this way of defining obscurity and attempted to reverse the term's negative connotations. In so doing they challenged the normative linguistic judgements which defined the term and questioned the authority of the literary tradition from which those judgements received their sanction.

The most important figure to be defended from the charge of obscurity at this time was Robert Browning. Browning was a significant choice for Swinburne and Pater because at this moment in his career he was on the point of achieving a long-wished-for respectability. After three decades of virtually complete critical neglect (itself a consequence of the reception of *Sordello* in 1840), Browning's reputation was in the process of becoming more assured. The publication of *Dramatis Personae* in 1864 together with the first part of *The Ring and the Book* in 1868 had secured for him serious attention; critics began to speak of Browning as a major poet – a prophet, ranked, though for quite different reasons, with Tennyson. In 1869, Robert Buchanan, for example, described *The Ring and the Book* as 'the most precious and profound spiritual treasure that England has produced since the days of Shakespeare';[1] and in periodicals as diverse as *The Christian Examiner*, *Chamber's Journal*, *Spectator*, *Cornhill Magazine* and *Saturday Review*, like-minded critics were unanimous in seeing *The Ring and the Book* as Browning's masterpiece, the culmination of his 'genius'.[2] Yet the old complaints, particularly those of inaccessibility and obscurity were still being made; indeed the sheer complexity of *The Ring and the Book* was main reason for their persistence. In this sense a particularly vituperative attack by Alfred Austin in the *Temple Bar* in 1869, only made explicit an old grievance.[3] Browning's work, Austin argued, was 'the very incarnation of discordant obscurity'; as such it barely deserved the name of poetry since it did not fulfil the fundamental function of poetry – that of communicating easily to an audience. It was precisely this controversial aspect of Browning's work – his esoteric vocabulary, unorthodox metre, non-standard syntax and so forth – which became the subject of enquiry for both Pater and Swinburne. They exploited for their own ends the ambivalence attaching to Browning's reputation in the late 1860s and early 1870s – they began to address, that is, the problem of assimilating an important but obscure poet to an established tradition of poetry. Unlike most of Browning's defenders, Swinburne and Pater expressed neither impatience nor perplexity at the obscurity of his writing;[4] rather, they simply reinterpreted Browning in such a way that obscurity became the most important defining feature of his work. In their hands Browning became the pattern of a literary stylist, commended for those qualities of innovation and singlemindedness which distinguished his work from that of his contemporaries.

Swinburne's defence of Browning took the form of a digression in his essay on George Chapman published in 1875.[5] He began by discriminating between two different phenomena, produced in turn by two different mental states. On the one hand there was 'genuine' obscurity which was pathological and very rare; it was 'the natural product of turbid forces and confused ideas; of a feeble and clouded or of a vigorous but unfixed and chaotic intellect'. (The examples Swinburne gave were Fulke Greville and George Chapman.) On the other hand, there was 'difficult' writing which was often, Swinburne suggested, erroneously labelled obscure by its critics. Such work was produced by the opposite kind of mental state, by 'decisive and incisive faculty of thought, . . . sureness and intensity of perception, . . . rapid and trenchant resolution of aim'. A prime example of this second mental state was to be found in the poetry of Robert Browning. Swinburne then argued that this 'obscurity' (which he renamed 'difficulty') was not an absolute quality of texts; it had to be understood in relation to a concept of audience. He suggested that those who claimed to find Browning's poetry difficult were merely revealing their own intellectual inadequacies. Browning was perfectly comprehensible to the like-minded – that is, to the intelligent and educated – reader, but never to what Swinburne called the 'ready reader':

> He is something too much the reverse of obscure; he is too brilliant and subtle for the ready reader of a ready writer to follow with any certainty the track of such an intelligence which moves with such incessant rapidity, or even to realise with what spider-like swiftness and sagacity his building spirit leaps and lightens to and fro . . . darts from centre and circumference of the glittering and quivering web of living thought woven from the inexhaustible stores of his perception and kindled from the inexhaustible fires of his imagination. He never thinks but at full speed; and the rate of his thought is to that of another man's as the speed of a railway to that of a waggon.[6]

Swinburne had valorised precisely the feature of Browning's work which Austin, and two decades of reviewers before him, had reviled. He had done so by reversing the terms of the argument. In

Swinburne's account of Browning, responsibility was shifted from
the poet to the reader. A difficult poem did not, as critics such as
Ruskin, Arnold and Austin had suggested, reflect adversely on the
poet; rather the audience had to 'read in a fit frame of mind . . . and
in the proper mood' – that is, 'not with . . . sluggish or sandblind eye
. . . but with open and pliant spirit, untired and undisturbed'.
Attention such as this would then ensure that the reader would:

> receive a vivid and active pleasure in following the swift and fine
> radiations, the subtle play and keen vibration of its sleepless fires; and
> the more steadily . . . trace their course . . . [and] see that these forked
> flashes of fancy and changing lights of thought move unerringly
> around one centre, and strike straight in the end to one point.[7]

Swinburne was proposing nothing less than a complete reversal of
the terms by which poetry – and by extension 'art' – was to be
evaluated. The assumption that literary art was to be judged by its
features was replaced by a theory of aesthetic perception; decisions
about what constituted 'good' poetry were determined not by the
existence of qualities in the work in question, but rather by the
'pleasure' afforded to the sensibility of the reader. The consequence
of privileging the special or educated readers, blessed with such
sensibilities, was to suggest that the worth of poetry increased in
accordance with the degree to which its audience was *restricted*; good
poetry was, by Swinburne's definition, highly élitist.

These proposals were in fact only making explicit the consequences of the argument concerning 'aesthetic criticism' earlier
proposed by Walter Pater in the 'Preface' to *The Renaissance*.[8] In
that 'Preface', Pater also argued that the value of works of art resided
not in any specific features, but rather in the 'degree of pleasure'
they afforded to the critic possessing 'a certain kind of temperament'.[9]
There was, moreover, a further connection between Pater's and
Swinburne's work. In his essay, 'Winckelmann', first published in
1867, Pater had also referred to Browning's obscurity, and in terms
which were remarkably similar to those later employed by Swinburne. Pater cited 'the brilliant example of the poetry of Robert
Browning' as an illustration of the creative processes of 'genius',
arguing that the difficulty or obscurity of Browning's poetry was
only the natural and inevitable consequence of artistic integrity:

> To discriminate that moment, to make it appreciable to us, that we
> may 'find' it, what a cobweb of allusions, what double and treble

reflexions of the mind upon itself, what an artificial light is constructed and broken over the whole chosen situation. . . . Yet in spite of this intricacy, the poem has a clear ring of a central motive. We receive from it the impression of one imaginative tone, of a single creative act. . . . To produce . . . [such effects] requires all the resources of poetry, language in its most purged form, its remote associations, its double and treble lights.[10]

Whatever local influences which may have operated between Pater and Swinburne, the fact that both covertly introduced discussions of Browning into unusual contexts – a critical study of an Elizabethan dramatist and an essay on an eighteenth-century German art-historian – taken with the fact that both defended him in similar ways (even using the same metaphors of light and optics) suggests a common, if submerged set of concerns.[11]

The main significance of this 'use' of Browning by Swinburne and Pater, however, is that both quite deliberately chose to define themselves in relation to a figure who was outside their circle and who had virtually no sympathies with their ambitions for art. In his famous exchange with Ruskin over the latter's allegations of obscurity in the 1850s, Browning had declared he would be 'disconcerted and apprehensive when the public, critics and all, begin to understand and approve me'.[12] However, by the late 1860s Browning had shown a marked willingness to revise his poetry in accordance with demands for clarity; the 1863 edition of *Sordello*, for example, incorporated some several thousand changes.[13] Browning was clearly ready to compromise in order to achieve a wider audience and greater accessibility. Indeed his amicable relationship with the Browning Society (whose primary intention was the popularisation of his work) is further evidence that he desired a greater clarity, and therefore the larger general readership which would have been the inevitable consequence.[14] In these senses, the Browning of Swinburne and Pater is little more than a cipher, used in the service of an argument with which he had little or no sympathy. Such an observation, however, provokes an important question. Why did these writers choose to defend a *non*-avant-garde poet?

One reason for this unusual strategy has to do with the intellectual conservatism of Britain; as I have suggested, it ensured that oppositional writers had to be circumspect, more covert in their activities than their French avant-garde contemporaries. In this sense, it is not surprising that Swinburne's discussion of Browning's obscurity was more comprehensive, and more explicit in its polemic, than Pater's earlier brief and allusive comments: the intellectual conditions in 1867 were quite different from those which obtained in 1875. But there was another, more 'positive' reason for defending Browning; it dramatically exposed the limitations of accepted or traditional definitions of art and literature. These definitions had never addressed the possibility of an avant-garde – indeed, as I have suggested, they necessarily excluded or marginalised innovative work. Nominally, however, Victorian nostrums about poetry should have embraced precisely the view of the poet as moralist and teacher, a role which Browning had to all intents and purposes achieved by the 1870s. That these definitions to some extent could not accommodate Browning's work was made abundantly clear by Pater's and Swinburne's need to 'reinterpret' him. Pater and Swinburne were thus able, for what were in their eyes quite legitimate reasons, to appropriate a conventional figure in order to challenge established orthodoxies. (In the late 1860s Browning was, after all, neither young, nor new, nor in his politics particularly controversial.) Such a strategy had the useful consequence of enlisting Browning as an ally in order to authorise unconventional activities. The paradox of this use of Browning lies, then, in the fact that he was *not* considered an avant-garde figure. In adopting this strategy of opposition to literary and artistic orthodoxies, Swinburne and Pater set a pattern for the activities of later nineteenth-century British avant-gardes. As I shall argue in subsequent chapters, other appropriations of traditional or eminent figures, especially those by Wilde, were to be much more ambitious: they included Shakespeare, Leonardo and Plato. Indeed whole areas of literary history would be redefined in precisely this way in order to authorise avant-garde theories and practices.

A much less well-known figure defended against charges of obscurity in the 1870s was the minor poet and doctor, Thomas Gordon Hake. For Rossetti, who reviewed a volume of Hake's poetry in 1871, the problem of obscurity in his work was exactly that of Browning's but on a miniature scale.[15] Hake's poetry was, according to Rossetti, a 'remote and reticent medium', sure to alienate him from the 'general reader'. His language was 'too frequently vague to excess', and his use of formal structures was 'preserved at the expense of meaning' and by 'baffling involutions . . . of diction'. Rossetti, however, was prepared to overlook such shortcomings because of Hake's obvious originality and sincerity, qualities which Rossetti acknowledged would be recognised only by what he called the 'fit reader' – by those few who were capable of looking 'past the author's difficulties to the spirit which shines through them'. (It is worth noticing that some years later, in 1900, Lionel Johnson used a similar phrase to describe Pater's appeal: 'If he died "leaving great" prose "unto a little clan" of appreciators, "a little clan" sure of increase and of successors, *satis est*, for him as for them.') [16] Hake's stylistic complexity was thus comprehensible only to an intellectual and cultural élite. But in a surprising twist to his argument Rossetti suggested that Hake could nevertheless be located within the main tradition of English poetry:

> It appears to us then that Dr. Hake is, in relation to his own time, as original a poet as one can well conceive possible. He is uninfluenced by any styles or mannerisms of the day to so absolute a degree as to tempt one to believe that the latest English singer he may even have heard of is Wordsworth; while in some respects his ideas and points of view are newer than the newest in vogue; and the external affinity frequently traceable to elder poets only throws this essential independence into startling and at times almost whimsical relief. His style, at its most characteristic pitch, is a combination of extreme homeliness, as of Quarles or Bunyan, with a formality and even occasional courtliness of diction which recall Pope himself in his most artificial flights; while one is frequently reminded of Gray by sustained vigour of declamation. This is leaving out of the question the direct reference to classical models which is perhaps in reality the chief source of what this poet has in common with the 18th century writers. [17]

Hake was to be rescued or rehabilitated albeit on highly élitist grounds, for his audience had been restricted to only those 'fit readers'. But Rossetti's artistic Midrash had also reinterpreted Hake; he was, in Rossetti's view, a literary stylist, and, like the reinterpreted Browning, could be assimilated into a literary tradition whose members were also, above all else, innovative stylists.

Rossetti's defence of Hake was more than log-rolling for a friend; following the publication of his own *Poems* in the previous year Rossetti too had been accused of obscurity. At the time he had been defended from these charges by Swinburne, although the extravagant language of Swinburne's review was less than helpful. Indeed it was one of the sources which provoked Robert Buchanan's famous attack on 'The Fleshly School of Poetry' which parodied, among other things, Swinburne's effusive aquatic metaphors.[18] In 1881 the appearance of Rossetti's revised *Poems* and his *Ballads and Sonnets* provoked the same criticism, but this time he found a more subtle and able apologist in the still relatively unknown Walter Pater. Pater had been invited to contribute an introductory essay on Rossetti to preface the selection of his poems which were to be included in the multi-volume *The English Poets* edited by T. H. Ward, Matthew Arnold's son-in-law, and published by Macmillan.[19] Pater argued, in a manner similar to his discussion of Browning, that Rossetti's obscurity was the necessary consequence of artistic integrity:

> His own meaning was always personal and even recondite, in a certain sense learned and casuistical, sometimes complex or obscure; but the term always, one could see, deliberately chosen from many competitors, as the just transcript of that peculiar phase of soul which he alone knew, precisely as he knew it.[20]

He then suggested that the appeal of such poetry could only be 'to a special and limited audience'. But he conceded that this was not a new state of affairs; 'it is well to remember', Pater argued, 'that [Thomas] Gray too . . . seemed in his own day, seemed even to [Samuel] Johnson, obscure'. Finally, Pater located Rossetti's poetry within a literary tradition, the defining feature of which was originality:

> In Rossetti at least [artifice is] redeemed by a seriousness of purpose, by that sincerity of his, which allies itself readily to a serious beauty, a sort of grandeur of literary workmanship – to a great style. One seems to hear there a really new kind of poetic utterance, with effects which have nothing else like them; as there is nothing else, for instance, like the narrative of Jacob's Dream, or Blake's design of the Singing of the Morning Stars, or Addison's Nineteenth Psalm.[21]

Beneath these attempts to redefine and revalue obscurity a set of political judgements was in operation. In each case, the defence of obscurity involved endorsing a form of élitism. Such a position may, of course, seem a highly conservative one, evidence that writers such as Swinburne, Pater and Rossetti were far from oppositional – in fact the contrary is true. To argue for any kind of literary élitism in Britain in the 1870s and 1880s was a highly subversive act, one which engaged with a contentious political issue. In general terms, this issue concerned the civilising and educative role which culture was thought by Victorian society to possess; more specifically, it had to do with the social and cohesive function of literature within that culture. From the early decades of the century the primary value of literature had been seen to reside in the moral knowledge which it embodied, as in John Stuart Mill's succinct definition: 'poetry, when it is really such, is truth'.[22] It was this view of literature which in turn had led critics such as Arnold to insist that literary style should be characterised by a 'clearness' and a 'simplicity'.[23] The assumption behind such views was that there existed a necessary relationship between language, thought and truth. So, for example, Herbert Spencer, in 'The Philosophy of Style', could argue that:

> Regarding language as an apparatus of symbols for the conveyance of thought, we may say that, as a mechanical apparatus, the more simple and better arranged its parts, the greater will be the effect produced.[24]

A similar proposition had been put forward by Mill in *A System of Logic: Ratiocinative and inductive*;[25] and in 'The Two Kinds of Poetry', he argued a case for the superiority of the 'logician-poet':

> Where, as in Milton, or to descend to our own time, in Coleridge, a poetic nature has been united with logical and scientific culture, the peculiarity of association arising from the finer nature so perpetually alternates with the associations attainable by commoner natures trained to high perfection, that its own particular law is not so conspicuously characteristic of the result produced, as in a poet like Shelley, to whom systematic intellectual culture, in a measure proportioned to the intensity of his own nature, had been wanting. Whether the superiority will naturally be on the side of the 'logician-poet' or of the mere poet – whether the writings of the one ought, as a whole, to be truer, and their influence more beneficent, than those of the other – is too obvious in principle to need statement.[26]

And it was precisely the same kind of argument which lay behind Benjamin Jowett's general complaint in 1876, made in the context of a discussion of Plato in his edition of *The Republic*:

> There are many passages in some of our greatest modern poets which are far too obscure; in which there is no proportion between style and subject; in which any half-expressed figure, any harsh construction, any distorted collocation of words, any remote sequence of ideas is admitted. . . . The obscurities of early Greek poets arose necessarily out of the state of language and logic which existed in their age. . . . For us the use of language ought in every generation to become clearer and clearer.[27]

To defend obscure or difficult writing as Swinburne, Rossetti and

Pater had done was to call into question the nature of this
relationship between language, thought and truth (and specifically,
moral knowledge); for, according to these writers, it was the
'recondite' nature of literary language, rather than its clarity and
simplicity, which ensured truthfulness, although they had, of
course, redefined the concept of truth. The proposition that truth
was apprehended through obscure, or 'private' languages also
implied that truth (or morality) must itself be a private or individual
matter. To defend obscurity was therefore to undermine two
orthodoxies: the assumption that language and literature had a social
and cohesive function; and the assumption that morality had
principally a social basis. The conservative reviewer, William John
Courthope, cogently summed up the issues:

> [Obscurity] indicates a failure on the part of the poet to recognise the
> nature of the conditions of his art. The poet did not originate the
> language in which he writes; he did not originate the thought and
> feeling to which he appeals. He finds himself set down in the midst of
> limitations, *natural and social*, of his own liberty; and if, instead of
> adapting himself to these, he endeavours to fight them, he mistakes
> the capacities of his instrument.[28]

These underlying political judgements explain the seriousness
with which obscurity was treated by critics in the 1880s and 1890s
compared to its treatment in the 1850s or 1860s. The targets of such
allegations tended to be the Aesthetes in general and Rossetti in
particular. In contrast to earlier criticisms of Browning obscurity
was now explained in two quite different ways, both of which were
directly related to the attempts by Swinburne, Pater and Rossetti to
redefine the concept of obscurity in the 1870s.[29] The first kind of
explanation saw obscurity as evidence of the emptiness of the poet's
thoughts. Simply put, obscure writing expressed 'nothing' and so
relinquished any claim to be literature. In 1882 in the *Edinburgh
Review*, for example, Henry Statham explained the obscurity of
Rossetti's poetry in the following way:

> The majority of the sonnets [are] . . . characterised by an arduous
> emptiness [,] . . . we turn over most of them with an increasing sense
> of their intellectual barrenness and weakness, of the preponderance of
> mere sound over meaning, the prevalence of an elaborate and cloying
> mannerism of words and metaphors, which seems not so much the
> expression of fullness of thought as the arrangement of elaborate
> drapery to hide the tenuity of meaning.[30]

The same year in the *Fortnightly Review*, Grant Allen made a similar argument. Noting that 'the most immature, or crudest, or most truly purposeless of our great writers' tended to produce the 'most amorphous and least definite or categorical in thinking and philosophising', he then described the difference between:

> [a] nebulous hazy thinker, who cloaks platitudes or unintelligible sayings in that grand, eloquent, high-souled phraseology [and] . . . the men who assert a definite idea in definite language.[31]

The example Allen gave of the first kind of thinker was Swinburne; and the latter was in his eyes best represented by figures such as Mill and Tennyson.

A second, and different, explanation of obscurity suggested that obscure writing in fact expressed immoral and therefore inappropriate thoughts. Moreover, such writing was often seen to be pathological in origin. This second explanation was usually only alluded to, or only made partly explicit. Thus, for example, John Campbell Shairp, in an essay entitled 'Aesthetic Poetry' in the *Contemporary Review*, noted, once more in reference to Rossetti's poetry, 'the subtleties and out-of-the-way thoughts and over-driven metaphors, which darken the meaning of many of the poems.' He also remarked on the 'atmosphere which is strange, and certainly not bracing – the fragrances . . . of musk and incense rather than heather and mountain thyme' which pervaded them. He concluded:

> [his] sonnets not only express, but brood over thoughts and imaginations which should not be expressed, or even dwelt upon in secret thought. Not all the subtle association or elaboration of words, nor dainty imagery in which they are dressed, can hide or remove the intrinsic earthiness that lies at the heart of them.[32]

Although they were different, both kinds of explanation arrived at broadly the same conclusions: first, and fundamentally, obscure writing could not make any claim to be literature; and second, the pervasiveness of obscurity among contemporary writers was a sign of 'decay' or decadence. For a critic such as Allen, this sense of decay was defined narrowly in terms of the demise of a set of linguistic standards; but for a figure such as Shairp, it signified a more general moral decadence. In his eyes, the obscurity which characterised the work of the Aesthetes was inextricably associated with corruption.

A further dimension to the debates about obscurity in the 1880s was provided by the rise of British nationalism. Nationalism gave a new significance to arguments about the social and cohesive function of literature, for a literary tradition was assigned the specific function of preserving a national identity. There were two main ways in which the concept of the 'literary' was redefined in order to accommodate nationalist ideas. First, the general moral knowledge which literature was held to embody was defined more narrowly to include those moral attributes deemed peculiarly or predominantly English (English in this instance was virtually synonymous with British); and second, the set of linguistic norms came to be seen as the defining features of the 'noble English style'. So, for example, Shairp, reviewing Ward's *The English Poets* in 1881, argued that:

> The poetry of England is the bloom of her national life. It contains the essence, expressed in the most beautiful form, of whatever is highest and deepest, most vivid and most pathetic, in the thoughts and sentiments which have swayed our countrymen during the successive ages of their history.[33]

In the 1880s, then, literary works tended to be partly seen in terms of the way in which they might contribute to the construction of this national literary heritage. The task of the reviewer was to 'explain their contents, or to indicate the relation of the poet's habit of thought and feeling to the ideas which Englishmen are accustomed to trust and admire'.[34] So, once again, it was possible for Shairp to issue the following advice at the conclusion to his essay on 'Aesthetic Poetry':

> If future poets wish to win the ear of their countrymen, and to merit the honour accorded to the highest poetry, they would be wise to cultivate manlier thought and nobler sentiment, expressed in purer and fresher diction, and to make their appeal . . . to the broader and healthier sympathies of universal man.[35]

In order for literary texts to fulfil this nationalist function – for them to be able to embody national characteristics – they had to have a social dimension; the reception of literature by Swinburne's category of 'ready readers' had to be unproblematic. However, the élitism implied by the defence of obscurity in terms of its expressive functions had explicitly problematised such notions. By implying that the basis of language and morality was private rather than social, Swinburne, Rossetti and Pater had effectively attempted to disable both the assumption that a set of common characteristics and values existed, and the argument that literature could transmit those national characteristics and values. In their view, the 'literary' and the 'national' could not be assimilated to each other simply because the former was predicated upon a notion of specificity or uniqueness.

Central to the attempts to redefine and revalue obscurity, then, was an attempt to redefine the concept of the 'literary', a process which in turn allowed traditions to be redefined. It is this activity which signals the importance of the debates about obscurity; they are the first indication that intellectual conditions had changed in Britain to the extent that it was possible to question traditions in a fundamental way, and that the relationship between the innovative writer and the past had, for the first time, become problematised. They are evidence, in other words, that the necessary preconditions for avant-garde activities obtained in Britain.

Notes

1. Robert Buchanan, *The Athenaeum*, (20 March 1869), 399. Quoted in Ezzat Abdulmajeed Khattab, 'The critical reception of Browning's *The Ring and the Book*: 1868–1889 and 1951–1968', *Salzburg Studies in English Literature*, 66 (1977), 10.
2. See Khattab, 25.
3. Alfred Austin, 'The poetry of the period', *Temple Bar*, 26 (1869), 316–33. Austin's criticism of Browning needs to be seen in the context of a larger polemic he was waging against 'The poetry of the period', the title he gave to his 1870 collection of essays critical of figures such as Tennyson, Swinburne, Emerson, Whitman and, significantly, Buchanan. See William Whitla, 'Browning, Alfred Austin, and the Byron Scandal', *Browning Society Notes*, 7 (1977), 12–32.
4. See, for example, the review of Browning in the *Spectator*, 28 (1855), 1346–7, in which he was described as possessing 'a fine mind enfeebled by caprice and want of discipline, and a true poet defrauding himself of fame, and the public of pleasure and improvement, by affectations, and puerilities'. The review then suggested that 'all these faults seem to us attributable either to the low vanity of attaining the praise of originality by the cheap method of being different from other people, or the inexcusable laziness of not choosing the trouble to correct his first thoughts.' Quoted in Boyd Litzinger and Donald Smalley (eds.), *Browning: The critical heritage* (London: Routledge and Kegan Paul, 1970), 164. For details of similar views, see Khattab, 16–17.
5. Algernon Charles Swinburne, *George Chapman* (London: Macmillan, 1875). The digression on Browning is reprinted in Clyde K. Hyder (ed.), *Swinburne as Critic* (London: Routledge and Kegan Paul, 1972), 156–63.

6. Hyder, 157.
7. Ibid.
8. Walter Pater, *The Renaissance*, ed. Donald Hill (Berkeley, Ca.: University of California Press, 1980), xix–xxv. Pater's correspondence with Macmillan suggests that the Preface was originally composed some time before 1872. Hill surmises that it was taken from an essay which later became 'The School of Giorgione', published first in 1877.
9. Ibid. xxi.
10. Ibid. 170–1. Paul Tucker has also been intrigued by the incongruous reference to Browning in 'Winckelmann'. He has, however, provided a quite different explanation of it. See Paul Tucker, 'Browning, Pater and the Hellenic Ideal', *Browning Society Notes*, 9 (1979), 2–7.
11. Pater returned to the subject of Browning's obscurity in 1887 in a review of Arthur Symons's *An Introduction to the Study of Browning* for *The Guardian*. There he argued (more comprehensively) that 'so intellectual a poet (and only the intellectual poet, as we have pointed out, can be adequate to modern demands) will have his difficulties. They were a part of the poet's choice of vocation, and he was fully aware of them.' See Walter Pater, *Essays from 'The Guardian'* (London: Macmillan, 1906), 41–51.
12. See Browning's letter to John Ruskin of 10 December 1855, in W. G. Collingwood, *The Life and Work of John Ruskin*, 2 vols. (London: Methuen, 1893), I, 200.
13. See Morse Peckham, 'Thoughts on Editing *Sordello*', *Studies in Browning and his Circle*, 5 (1977), 11–18.
14. See William S. Peterson, *Interrogating the Oracle: A history of the London Browning Society* (Athens, Ohio: Ohio University Press, 1969).
15. See Dante Gabriel Rossetti, '*Madeline* with other Poems and Parables. By Thomas Gordon Hake, M.D., *Academy*, (1 Feb 1871), 105–7.
16. See Lionel Johnson, 'For A Little Clan', *Academy*, (13 October 1900). Reprinted in Lionel Johnson, *Post Liminium*, ed. T. Whittemore (London: Elkin Matthews, 1911), 18.
17. Rossetti, 107.
18. See Swinburne, 'The Poems of Dante Gabriel Rossetti', *Fortnightly Review*, 7 n.s. (1870), 551–79; and Robert Buchanan, 'The Fleshly School of Poetry: Mr D.G. Rossetti', *Contemporary Review*, 18 (1871), 334–50. Swinburne described Rossetti's style in the following terms:

> He is too great a master of speech to incur the blame of hard or tortuous expression; and his thought is too sound and pure to be otherwise dark than as a deep well-spring at noon may be even where the sun is strongest and brightest. In its furthest depth there is nothing of weed or of mud; whatever of haze may seem to quiver there is a weft of the sun's spinning, a web not of woven darkness but of molten light.

Buchanan parodied it thus:

> The mind of Mr. Rossetti is like a glassy mere, broken only by the dive of some water-bird or the hum of winged insects, and brooded

over by an atmosphere of insufferable closeness, with a light blue sky
above it, sultry depths mirrored within it, and a surface so thickly
sown with water-lilies that it retains its glassy smoothness even in the
strongest wind.

19. Walter Pater, 'Dante Gabriel Rossetti' in *The English Poets*, vol. 4, ed.
T. H. Ward (London: Macmillan, 1894), 633–41. The essay was later
reprinted in Walter Pater, *Appreciations* (London: Macmillan, 1889).
20. Ibid. 634.
21. Ibid. 636.
22. John Stuart Mill, 'Thoughts on poetry and its varieties', *Collected Works
of John Stuart Mill*, I, eds. John M. Robson and Jack Stillinger
(London: University of Toronto Press, 1981a), 346. See also John
Morley *On the Study of Literature* (Edinburgh: R. and C. Clark, 1887):

Literature consists of all the books – and there are not so many – where
moral truth and human passion are touched with a certain largeness,
sanity, and attraction of form. . . . Poets, dramatists, humourists, satirists,
masters of fiction, the great preachers, the character writers, the maxim-
writers, the great political orators – they are all literature in so far as they
teach us to know man and to know human nature.'

23. Matthew Arnold, 'Preface to first edition of *Poems* (1853)', *Matthew
Arnold: Selected poems and prose*, ed. Miriam Allott (London: J. M.
Dent, 1978), 139. See also Arthur Tilley, 'Two Theories of Poetry',
Macmillan's Magazine, 44 (1881), 277:

There [must be] no undue attention to detail, no striving after
startling effects, no breathlessness, no excitement; over the whole
presides perfect self-restraint and moderation. . . . But of course self-
restraint implies much more than mere brevity; it implies restraint of
thought, restraint of power, restraint of imagery.

24. Herbert Spencer, 'The Philosophy of Style', *Essays: Scientific, political,
theological* (London: Williams and Norgate, 1868), 11.
25. John Stuart Mill, *A System of Logic: Ratiocinative and inductive*, 2 vols.
(London: John W. Parker, 1848).
26. Mill, 'The Two Kinds of Poetry', *The Monthly Repository*, (1833). The
essay was later revised to form part of 'Thoughts on poetry and its
varieties'. See *Collected Works*, I, 364. I quote from the form of the
earlier essay.
27. Benjamin Jowett, *The Republic of Plato* (Oxford: Clarendon Press,
1876), 1.
28. William John Courthope, ' "Jocoseria" and the critics: A plea for the
reader', *National Review*, 1 (1883b), 552 (emphasis added). Courthope
followed this general statement with some specific examples. He
argued:

The greatest poets show by their practice that they are perfectly
aware of this truth; they take their materials from the society about
them. In the *Iliad*, the *Aeneid*, and *Paradise Lost*, the ground-work of

the story is not the invention of the poet, but a tradition or belief of the people. And even in the parts of their work which are entirely inventive, there is never a sentiment put forward by these poets, or by the characters which they create, that does not correspond with some idea pre-existent in the minds of the readers. The same, in a greater or less degree, is true of the Greek tragedians, the Elizabethan dramatists, and the greatest lyrical poets of all nations, who invariably appeal to some simple and universal feeling in the human mind.

29. Browning's obscurity was still an issue in the 1880s and 1890s, although generally the criticisms of him were not of the same kind as those which attached to the Aesthetes. In this respect, it is interesting to notice that the Browning Society dropped the subject of Browning's obscurity from their agenda in the mid–1880s, adopting instead the 'safer' ground of Browning's theology. William Peterson has noted the difficulty experienced by Frederick Furnivall at this time in trying to find a publisher for an essay by James Thompson on Browning's obscurity (Thompson's essay was refused by the *Fortnightly Review*, *Temple Bar*, *Contemporary Review* and *Fraser's Magazine*); and he speculates on the reasons for the mysterious omission from the society's publications of its proceedings of an essay also on obscurity by Ernest Radford. See Peterson, 59 and 146.

30. Henry Statham, 'Rossetti's Poems', *Edinburgh Review*, 155 (1882), 335. For similar views see also the unsigned review, 'Art V: The poetry of Rossetti', *British Quarterly*, 76 (1882), 109–27, which has the following note: '[It is due to the writer of this article to state that it was in the Editor's hands for publication early in the year, some weeks therefore before the publication of the April number of "The Edinburgh Review," which contains an article on Rossetti's poems agreeing in many respects with the views expressed above. – Ed. Brit. Quart.]'.

31. Grant Allen, 'The Decay of Criticism', *Fortnightly Review*, 37 (1882), 347.

32. John Campbell Shairp, 'Aesthetic poetry: Dante Gabriel Rossetti', *Contemporary Review*, 42 (1882a), 23.

33. John Campbell Shairp, 'English poets and Oxford critics', *Quarterly Review*, 153 (1882b), 431. This attempt to redefine the 'literary' on nationalist grounds was noted by Richard G. Moulton, a Cambridge and London extension lecturer and later Professor of English at Chicago University. In a report which he compiled and published privately in 1880 on 'The Reorganisation of Liberal Education', he devoted a lengthy section to literature and language where he described how the 'study of literature' had become a discrete and special activity, to be distinguished from the more traditional study of the classics:

It will not be seriously contended that the amount of Virgil, Xenophon, or Greek Testament they [Honours students] go through has a perceptible effect on their *literary* culture; an effect of a gymnastic kind it undoubtedly has, but this is only a variation of the effect of their other studies in Mathematics and Science. . . . Apart from gymnastic in what should literary culture consist? . . . In the possession of a body of common associations as materials for social intercourse; in the apprehension of a people's literature as a reflection of their national life . . . . How is it possible for the least approach to any of these results to be obtained by means of a Greek Play?

See Richard G. Moulton, *The Reorganisation of Liberal Education* (Cambridge: Leader and Sons, 1880), 17–18.

34. F. W. Myers, 'Rossetti and the religion of beauty', *The Cornhill Magazine*, 47 (1883), 213–240. Myers was not sympathetic to this practice, his view of Rossetti being very close to that of Pater:

We may note that his [Rossetti] sensitive and reserved individuality; his life, absorbed in Art, and aloof from – without being below – the circles of politics and fashion; his refinement, created as it were from within, and independent of conventional models, point him out as a member of that new aristocracy of which we have already spoken, that *optimacy* of passion and genius . . . which is coming into existence as a cosmopolitan gentility among the confused and fading class-distinctions of the past. (222)

35. Shairp, 'Aesthetic Poetry', 32.

CHAPTER 5

Walter Pater:
The 'rehabilitation' of tradition

W hen a literary avant-garde did finally emerge in Britain from the intellectual disquiet of the 1870s, it did so covertly, its polemic submerged in the respectable discourse of literary criticism. Moreover, a significant proportion of the work which that avant-garde singled out for comment was not by foreign avant-gardes and writers; rather, paradoxically, it was by figures who in Britain were considered to be eminent, orthodox, and to some extent even traditional. Whatever its sympathies with France and with certain French writers, the British literary avant-garde was careful not to align itself too closely with the revolutionary rhetoric of French avant-gardism. Instead it chose to rehearse its unconventional theories of art and literature by means of an apparently conventional device – by adopting the conventional practice of literary criticism and by discussion of conventional or traditional figures.

From the very outset then, the strategies of opposition to the past developed by figures such as Pater, Morris and Wilde, in recognition of the very different intellectual climate in which they were situated, were to subvert from within rather than revolutionise; to use, but to undermine through that use, existing concepts and categories of thought, rather than attempt to replace them on a wholesale basis. One of the clearest illustrations of these attitudes towards the past, tradition and the innovative artist in Pater's *oeuvre* is to be found in his short 'Introduction' to Charles Lancelot Shadwell's translation of *The Purgatory*, published in 1892.[1] In that 'Introduction', in a manner similar to his treatment of Browning nearly two decades earlier, Pater took advantage of a contemporary uncertainty over the

98

nature of Dante's historical significance – of his place, that is, in a literary tradition.[2] In the opening paragraphs Pater compares neglect of Dante in the past with attempts in the nineteenth century to rehabilitate his work:

> He too had to pass through ages with no natural ear for him; while it is only the good fortune of the present generation that its turn for eclecticism, removing prejudice, has fitted it for a really intelligent and critical study of Dante's work, encouraged for its reward therein by certain special aspects of Dante's genius which are in close kinship with its own.[3]

Pater goes on to elaborate on the precise nature of Dante's kinship with the nineteenth century – the affinities which he has with what Pater elusively calls contemporary 'tendencies'. These affinities, however, turn out to be somewhat different from those generally expected from such a historical analogy; they are not of 'sentiment' nor of 'politics' nor of 'religious faith'. On the contrary, in all these ways Dante was 'remote and strange'. It is the attitude which he adopted towards his subject matter which, in Pater's eyes, marks Dante's significance for the nineteenth century:

> He [Dante] has handled on a grand scale the grandest of subjects, in a way which after all fair comparison must be declared unique, and so as to make it his own – that immense intellectual deposit of thirteen believing centuries – with a generous outlay of himself, of his own richly endowed and richly cultivated personality, of what is intimate and peculiar in it. On a scrupulous orthodoxy he has impressed a deep personal originality.[4]

According to Pater, Dante's 'genius' – his 'independence' – lay in his recognition that, whatever the nature of his subject matter, it was necessary 'to treat it as a literary artist, to charm his reader . . . [by] a command of every sort of minute literary beauty, an expressiveness, a care for style and rhythm at every point.' The grounds for Dante's assimilation into a literary tradition appropriate for the nineteenth century lay, Pater argues, in his originality of style. The contemporary 'tendencies' which he prefigures (and therefore also authorises) turn out to be those of, what else? – Aestheticism – and more specifically, of Pater himself.

Pater's use of Dante here is a clear example of both aspects of his strategy of opposition to contemporary literary orthodoxies. The first of these, discussed briefly in the previous chapter, concerns his endorsement of stylistic originality: his argument that artistic integrity necessitates the creation of a personal or private language. As I have suggested, the valorisation of artistic innovation on these particular grounds was a highly subversive one, for the sanction of linguistic obscurity, and thus of élitism, undermined the social and cohesive functions then commonly predicated of literature. In his essay 'Style', published in *Appreciations* (1889), Pater returned to the issues which he had raised apropos of Browning and Rossetti.[5] Pater began the essay by presenting his view of the nature of literary art:

> The writer's aim . . . comes to be the transcribing, not of the world, not of mere fact, but of his sense of it, he becomes an artist, his work *fine* art; and good art . . . in proportion to the truth of his presentiment of that sense. . . . Truth! there can be no merit, no craft at all, without that. And further, all beauty is in the long run only *fineness* of truth, or what we call expression, the finer accommodation of speech to that vision within.[6]

Pater then describes the exact process of the transcription, or 'representation' of 'soul-fact', and he does so in terms which appear to the unobservant reader to be uncompromisingly conservative. For Pater stresses precisely those qualities of restraint, sincerity, craftsmanship and, above all, respect for a medium, which had been insisted upon by critics as otherwise diverse as William Courthope, Matthew Arnold and Benjamin Jowett. He claims that 'the literary artist is of necessity a scholar, and in what he proposes to do will have in mind, first of all, the scholar and the scholarly conscience.' The reason that Pater gives is that 'the material in which he works is no more a creation of his own than the sculptor's marble'. However, the idea that Pater may be making any significant concession to linguistic orthodoxies is an illusion; for he proceeds to discuss a writer's 'freedom' with language in a manner which totally subverts those conservative orthodoxies he had invoked:

> A writer, full of matter he is before all things anxious to express, may think of those laws, the limitations of vocabulary, structure, and the like, as a restriction, but if a real artist will find in them an opportunity. . . . He will feel the obligation not of the laws only, but of those affinities, avoidances, those mere preferences, of his language. . . . He is really vindicating his liberty in the making of a vocabulary, an entire system of composition, for himself, his own true manner. . . . He does but show his intelligence to the rules of language in his freedoms with it. . . . He begets a vocabulary faithful to the colouring of his own spirit, and in the strictest sense original.[7]

In defining the 'literary' in the 'Style' essay, Pater had employed exactly the same terms as his contemporaries, and he had identified the idea of 'truth' in literature with qualities such as restraint and craftsmanship. However, the effect of his so doing was to expose the epistemological assumptions of that original proposition. In Pater's view 'literary truth' ('truth . . . as expression, that finest and most intimate form of truth, the vraie vérité') far from demanding adherence to a national style, provided the justification for its opposite, a stylistic eclecticism: 'employing for its one sole purpose – the absolute accordance of expression to idea – all other literary beauties and excellences whatever: how many kinds of style it covers, explains, justifies, and at the same time safeguards!'[8] Indeed in an explicit reference to the philosophical assumptions concerning the relationship between linguistic clarity and truth which lay beneath those arguments, Pater enlists as an authority for his understanding of that relationship the Oxford philosopher and cleric Henry Mansel. According to Pater, Mansel 'wrote a book, of fascinating precision . . . to show that all the technical laws of logic are but means of securing, in each and all of its apprehensions, the unity, the strict identity with itself, of the apprehending mind.' Pater then compares Mansel's claims with his own view of language, arguing that:

> all the laws of good writing aim at a similar unity or identity of the mind in all the processes by which the word is associated to its import. The term is right, and has its essential beauty, when it becomes, in a manner, what it signifies, as with the names of simple sensations.'[9]

The text which Pater had in mind was probably Mansel's *Prolegomena Logica* which attempts to demonstrate the necessary relationship between logic and psychology. Mansel's argument was based upon a commonplace distinction between 'thought', a mediated process subject to universal laws, of which logic was the study; and 'intuitions', individual and unmediated acts of perception which were the province of psychology. His originality lay, however, in his suggestion that the two were necessarily related: the latter was required to confirm the 'actual' (as opposed to necessary or possible) truth of the concepts and judgements of the former. Logic, or 'pure thought' had, in other words, 'to be guaranteed by the testimony of this or that special experience'. However, most appealing to Pater's aesthetic was probably Mansel's view that language belonged to the realm of intuition rather than to thought: 'words are not the signs of thoughts', Mansel argued, 'but of intuitions'. Despite this apparent congruence of Mansel's views with Pater's idea of literary expression, Mansel's religious convictions in fact made him a rather odd authority; indeed Pater's appropriation of Mansel required him to overlook some of the later writing – particularly the neo-Kantian critique of J. S. Mill's epistemological relativism in *The Philosophy of the Conditioned* where Mansel attempted to demonstrate that human inability to conceive the Divine or Absolute did not mean that it did not exist.[10]

The 'Style' essay, although Pater's most cogent discussion of his concepts of literary expression and artistic innovation, was in fact only one of several occasions when he attempted to develop and defend the issues which had been raised in his passing comment on Browning in *The Renaissance*. In this respect it is worth glancing briefly at one other occasion when he rehearses these issues – the defence of Euphuism in Chapter VI of his novel, *Marius the Epicurean* (1885).

Euphuism, an ornate or affected style which Pater referred to as 'the minute culture of form', was criticised on two grounds in the nineteenth century. The first concerned mannerism and artificiality. As such, Euphuism was directly opposed to the usual prescriptions for clarity, simplicity and truth which constituted 'the pure style . . . simple, transparent, unloaded with ornament' and hence the 'fittest vehicle' of literary expression.[11] Euphuism, by contrast, was 'idle dilettantism'; as one critic memorably said of Rossetti, 'we always fancy [him] adorning himself with a lily – like Haydn with his dress suit and diamond ring – and calmly sitting down to manipulate the English language.'[12] The second criticism was that Euphuism carried with it a suggestion of 'falsehood' – more specifically, of 'unmanliness' or effeminacy; and was thus seen to be the 'accompaniment' of an 'unhealthy [or immoral] sentiment'.[13] Indeed, in his review of Ward's *English Poets* in 1882, John Campbell Shairp devoted a long section to the history of Euphuism, describing it as an Elizabethan 'contagion', the eradication of which had taken some 'two hundred years . . . before . . . simplicity became the inheritance of all Englishmen'.[14] Following the publication of *The Renaissance*, Pater's style had been noticed; he too had been accused of affectation, obscurity and effeminacy. In *Marius* the criticism directed at Flavian from 'certain elderly counsellors'

('Cannot those who have a thing to say, say it directly? Why not be simple and broad, like the old writers of Greece?')[15] can be read as a reference to these complaints. In reply Pater argues that Euphuism, despite its occasional 'fopperies and mannerisms', was in fact highly serious. Indeed for Marius the practice of Euphuism had a quasi-religious quality: with 'its fastidious sense of a correctness in external form', Euphuism was the work of a craftsman, representing those moments when 'the literary conscience has been awakened to forgotten duties towards language, towards the instrument of expression.'[16] The point to notice, however, is that the standards of correctness and craftsmanship invoked by Pater were quite different from those of writers such as Courthope. They did not, for example, imply obedience to a set of linguistic or stylistic rules – to a notional 'national style'. Rather, correctness entailed finding a language appropriate for the expression of individual intuitions. Pater described Flavian's Euphuism in the following terms:

> From the natural defects, from the pettiness, of his Euphuism, his assiduous cultivation of manner, he was saved by the consciousness that he had a matter to present, very real, at least to him. That preoccupation of the dilettante with what might seem mere details of form, after all did but serve the purpose of bringing to the surface, sincerely and in their integrity, certain strong personal intuitions, a certain vision or apprehension of things as really being, with important results, thus, rather than thus, – intuitions which the artistic or literary faculty was called upon to follow, with the exactness of wax or clay clothing the model within.[17]

Five years earlier, Pater had made a similar argument in his discussion of Shakespeare's 'delicate raillery' against Euphuism in *Love's Labour Lost*. Noting the tendency of Euphuism to 'foppery' and to making itself 'ridiculous' Pater nevertheless insisted that Euphuism could, and often did, have a 'curious charm' – 'a delightful side, a quality in no sense "affected," by which it satisfies a real instinct in our minds – the chance so many of us have for an exquisite and curious skill with words.' Pater's argument here, and more explicitly in *Marius*, was that correctly practised Euphuism represented a uniquely literary (and therefore a highly personal) attitude towards language. It was a quality present in some degree in all literary art. Pater's clearest example in *Marius* is Homer:

> And how poetic the simple incident seemed, told just thus! . . . One might think there had been no effort in it; that here was but the

almost mechanical transcript of a time, naturally, intrinsically, poetic
. . . . Or might the closer student discover even here, even in Homer,
the mediatorial function of the poet, as between the reader and the
actual matter of his experience. . . . Had Homer, even, appeared
unreal and affected in his poetic flight, to some people of his own age,
as seemed to happen with every new literature in turn?[18]

Homer, as Pater's reference to the 'old writers of Greece' makes
clear, was generally considered – like the 'best' of Shakespeare – to
exemplify a 'simple and broad' style. Pater's strategy here is a
familiar one: it involves appropriation and reinterpretation of a
traditional figure in such a way that that figure comes to represent,
and therefore also authorise, Pater's own subversive views on the
nature of literary expression.

Pater's second form of opposition to the past concerns an attitude
towards tradition. The issue, as he phrased it in *Marius*, was that of
'the intellectual situation . . . between the children of the present and
those earliest masters.' Presented in fictional terms, it was the
problem encountered by Flavian when he attempted to found a 'new
literary school' – the problem of 'the burden of precedent' whose
'overwhelming authority' seemed to 'leave no place . . . for novelty
or originality'.[19] Pater's method for resolving that opposition
between the innovative writer and the traditions 'all around one' was
to redefine traditions in such a way that an opposition was no longer
perceived to exist. To this end, Pater appropriated and reinterpreted
figures of proven and demonstrable eminence in order to exhibit the
inadequacy of existing definitions of a literary tradition and, once
again, to authorise his own redefinition of those traditions in terms
of stylistic innovation. Thus the literary tradition authorising
Aestheticism, though consisting of orthodox figures – Plato, Dante,
Leonardo, Shakespeare, Wordsworth and so forth – is in fact eclectic
in that it is defined in terms of style rather than national 'thoughts
and sentiments', or 'feelings and aspirations'. In this way Pater
silently elides the distinctions between 'the children of the present
and those earliest masters'.[20]

Although Pater's practice of finding antecedents and thus authority for contemporary avant-garde activities was highly subversive,
the idea that analogies could be fruitfully drawn between distant
historical events and the present was in fact fairly orthodox in the
nineteenth century. This figural or analogic reading of history had its
origins in scriptural typology, a method of Biblical and Talmudic

exegesis dating from the early Christian era which had been revitalised in the nineteenth century by Evangelical Anglicans. According to the typological exegesis which they advocated, the believer read the Bible in order to find foreshadowings or prefigurements of Christ. In general terms this process entailed seeing past events as structural prefigurings analogous to the present, and seeing present events in their turn prefiguring the future. So the truth of the New Testament could be confirmed by the prophecies of the Old, and the truth of the Old Testament prophecies were in turn guaranteed by the Truth of the Gospel. In this mirroring process, truth is finally confirmed not from evidence in the phenomenal world; it derives from a divine order which exists beyond time but is fulfilled within it. The idea of historical or biblical event as prefigurement was thus firmly teleological; and the providential view of history which it implied was, like the assumptions underlying Whiggish gradualism, a highly appealing one in so far as it provided a 'vision of history . . . deeply comforting to . . . restless natures of the late nineteenth century'.[21]

Typological exegesis informed the work of several of Pater's contemporaries, notably Ruskin and Carlyle, and more significantly, certain members of the Pre-Raphaelite Brotherhood.[22] However, by the last quarter of the nineteenth century, the authority of the Evangelical Anglicans and of scriptural typology had been undermined by advances in biblical criticism, comparative philology and geology: together their findings had demonstrated that the Bible could not be literally true.[23] However, while typology as scriptural exegesis may have suffered an eclipse, typology as 'a mode of thought . . . [which] leads to a theory of history, or more accurately of historical process'[24] survived, finding its most cogent expression in the identification by historians of certain currents in late nineteenth-century Victorian Britain with the history of ancient Rome.[25] That Pater was fully consonant with typological methods of reading history has already been established, and *Marius*, both in terms of its subject matter and structure, has usually been taken as the most obvious example of that familiarity.[26] However, Pater's use of typology (a conventional, moralising form) to find prefigurements of Aestheticism, suggests a more ambiguous and subversive attitude towards that method than most accounts have so far allowed.[27] The suggestion that history could yield analogies with a practice as corrupting as Aestheticism could be seen to undermine the providential premiss of typological or figural readings of history. It demonstrated the selective nature of those readings. (Indeed in 'Style', Pater had written: 'your historian, for instance, with absolutely truthful intention, amid the multitude of facts presented to him must needs select, and in selecting asserts some thing of his own humour[,] . . . moving full of poignant sensibility amid the records of the past . . . modify[ing] – who can tell where and to what degree?')[28] More importantly it implied that the past only existed as a construction by the present. The suggestion that the relationship between the past (or tradition) and the present was a dynamic one, that the present was as much a creator of traditions, as it was created by them, was made explicit in Pater's later writing, particularly, as William Shuter has argued, in his construction of a tradition of Platonic scholarship in *Plato and Platonism* into which his own criticism of Plato could be assimilated.[29] However, this process had already been hinted at in 'The Poetry of Michelangelo' in *The Renaissance*. There Pater had described the historical significance of the artist:

> That strange interfusion of sweetness and strength is not to be found in those who claimed to be his followers; but it is found in many of those who worked before him, and in many others down to our own time, in William Blake, for instance, and Victor Hugo, who, though not of his school, and unaware, are his true sons, and help us to understand him, as he in turn interprets and justifies them. Perhaps this is the chief use in studying old masters.[30]

At one level this passage seems to suggest a conventional typological reading where innovation in Michelangelo's work is seen as both prefiguring future artists and as having been prefigured in the work of distant predecessors. However, Pater also suggests that there is a sense in which later artists, such as Hugo and Blake, help to understand or interpret Michelangelo: their work determines the historical significance assigned to Michelangelo. It is this dialectic between past and present which, Pater claims, is the 'chief *use* in studying old masters.'

Apart from nineteenth-century uses of typology, Pater's prefigurative view of history also owed much to Plato and the concepts of metempsychosis (the transmigration of the soul) and anamnesis (the myth of pre-existence) elaborated in the *Meno*.[31] These Platonic ideas of antecedent knowledge, although they underlie much of Pater's earlier writing, were discussed most fully by him in *Plato and*

Platonism.[32] In the opening chapter Pater explains the course of intellectual history in terms of the doctrine of 'reminiscence' or recurrence, and he disputes the (then) usual view of Plato as the 'creator of philosophy . . . [whose] achievement may well seem an absolutely fresh thing in the morning of the mind's history':

> The thoughts of Plato, like the language he has to use . . . are covered with the traces of previous labour and have had their earlier proprietors. If at times we become aware in reading him of certain anticipations of modern knowledge, we are also quite obviously among the relics of an older, a poetic or half-visionary world. It is hardly an exaggeration that in Plato, in spite of his wonderful savour of literary freshness, there is nothing absolutely new: or rather, as in many other very original products of human genius, the seemingly new is old also, a palimpsest, a tapestry of which the actual threads have served before.[33]

All this has the making of a contradiction. Pater, in many other ways an avant-garde writer, appears here to compromise severely the idea of intellectual or artistic innovation. But in fact the contradiction may easily be explained. First it is clear that Pater did hold to some notion of originality. As I have suggested, in his 'Style' essay and in his comments on various individuals such as Rossetti, Dante and Browning, Pater constantly reiterates his belief in the necessity of originality or uniqueness of style. Indeed, even here in *Plato and Platonism* he repeats the point:

> Nothing but the life-giving principle of cohesion is new; the new perspective, the resultant complexion, the expressiveness which familiar thoughts attain by their novel juxtaposition. In other words, the *form* is new. But then, in the creation of philosophical literature, as in all other products of art, *form*, in the full signification of that word, is everything, and the mere matter is nothing.[34]

Second, it is equally true that Pater stressed the idea of recurrence or prefigurement; indeed, as William Shuter has argued, it is perhaps the rationale behind his own method of writing and his tendency to 'reshuffle' his texts. But such an argument also allowed Pater a sleight-of-hand: it allowed him to deny the novelty of his controversial arguments for stylistic originality – to imply that they were in fact traditional.

The importance of intertextuality in Pater's work, the pervasiveness of his borrowings from other writers and from his own earlier work, have already been noted by a number of critics, most recently

in relation to his subversion of certain forms of intellectual authority.[35]
The most significant aspect of this intertextuality concerns Pater's
systematic appropriation and reinterpretation – his term is 'rehabilitation' – of the work of eminent historical figures in order to confirm
his own views about a 'constant tradition' of literary art which
endorsed Aestheticism. In 'Style', for example, Pater invokes figures
as diverse as Livy, Tacitus, Cicero, Plato, Pascal, Milton, Michelet,
Blake, Scott, Newman, Schiller, Tennyson, Wordsworth, Flaubert,
Stendhal, Hugo, and even the English Bible, in order to support his
definition of the 'literary' in terms of stylistic originality. However,
some of his most ambitious and comprehensive 'rehabilitations' are
to be found in his earlier essays, particularly those on Leonardo and
Wordsworth.

Pater's comments on Leonardo appeared first in an essay entitled
'Notes on Leonardo da Vinci' in the *Fortnightly Review* in 1869, and
were later included in *The Renaissance*. Pater begins his account
of the artist in a manner which would later become familiar; he
notes the disagreements over the nature of Leonardo's 'genius',
particularly the revisions which Vasari made to *La vite de' più eccellenti
pittori, scultori ed architetti*, and to the discussion of Vasari's work in
the early nineteenth century. Pater's point, however, is that these
nineteenth-century debates possess little relevance for the aesthetic
critic who has to 'analyse for himself the impression made on him by
those works, and try to reach through it a definition of the chief
elements of Leonardo's genius'.[36] In light of this, it is therefore not
surprising that Pater should find in Leonardo precisely those
qualities valorised by Aestheticism:

> Other artists have been as careless of present or future applause, in
> self-forgetfulness, or because they set moral or political ends above
> the ends of art; but in him this solitary culture of beauty seems to have
> hung upon a kind of self-love, and a carelessness in the work of art of
> all but art itself. Out of the secret places of a unique temperament he
> brought strange blossoms and fruits hitherto unknown; and for him,
> that novel impression conveyed, the exquisite effect woven, counted
> as an end in itself – a perfect end.[37]

In fact, Pater's treatment of Leonardo is remarkably similar to his
later account of Dante's genius. Indeed Pater goes on to describe
Leonardo's singularity in terms of the attitude which he adopts
towards his subject-matter:

No one ever ruled over the mere *subject* in hand more entirely than Leonardo, or bent it more dexterously to purely artistic ends. And so it comes to pass that though he handles sacred subjects continually, he is the most profane of painters; the given person or subject . . . is often merely the pretext for a kind of work which carries one altogether beyond the range of its conventional associations. . . . We have seen him using incidents of sacred story, not for their own sake, or as mere subjects for pictorial realisation, but as a cryptic language for fancies all his own.[38]

The point is made more forcefully in reference to the *Last Supper*, where Pater describes Leonardo's method of painting as 'another effort to lift a given subject out of the range of its traditional associations'.[39] What Leonardo and Dante share is an exclusive preoccupation with style – with the representation of 'soul-fact'. It is precisely the personal, intimate, and above all *private* nature of this preoccupation which, according to Pater, liberates the artist and his work from the 'burden of precedent' – from 'traditional associations' and 'scrupulous' orthodoxies.

Other 'rehabilitations', following the pattern set in the account of Leonardo, are to be found in *Appreciations*. Their subjects include Wordsworth, Charles Lamb and Shakespeare. The most provocative of all these 're-writings' is Pater's appropriation of Wordsworth. 'On Wordsworth' was originally published in 1874. Its time of composition was therefore very close to the publication of *The Renaissance*, and the essay is in a sense an extended discussion of some of the issues which had been raised in that earlier work. Moreover, at this time, the reputation of Wordsworth, in the wake of the 1850 edition of *The Prelude*, was undergoing a revision; he was occasionally accused of being too philosophical, or as Mill so succinctly put it, 'compared with the greatest poets, he may be said to be the poet of unpoetical natures.'[40] As with Browning and Dante, Pater had chosen to redefine a poet whose contemporary significance had become a matter of dispute. The republication of the essay in *Appreciations* in 1889 was also timely, for by this time Wordsworth's reputation had revived; he was the 'Giant' which Shairp had described in his review of *The English Poets* in 1882. The consolidation of Wordsworth's reputation had owed much to Arnold's overt propagandising of him in the late 1870s, and in particular to his Introduction to a selection of Wordsworth's poems commissioned by Macmillan in 1877, and published separately in

Macmillan's Magazine in 1879.[41] Here Arnold had 'rescued' Wordsworth from critics such as Pater by arguing that he was, above all else, a moralist:

> We find attraction, . . . at times, in a poetry . . . where the contents may be what they will, but where the form is studied and exquisite. [But we] delude ourselves [,] . . . and the best cure for our delusion is to let our minds rest upon that great and inexhaustible word *life*. . . . A poetry of revolt against moral ideas is a poetry of revolt against *life*; a poetry of indifference towards moral ideas is a poetry of indifference towards life. . . . Where, then, is Wordsworth's superiority? It is here: he deals with . . . *life*, as a whole, . . . powerfully.[42]

The terms for discussing Wordsworth in the 1880s were quite different from those which had existed a decade earlier when Pater first published his essay. Indeed, it was Wordsworth who, more than any other poet, had been invoked as a model against which the stylistic aberrance of Pater (and Aestheticism) could be measured. Critics in the *British Quarterly*, *Edinburgh Review*, and *Contemporary Review*, had, in their attacks on Rossetti, Pater and Aestheticism, quoted from, or alluded to, Wordsworth as a moralist possessing a style of exemplary clarity.[43]

The principal aim of Pater's essay on Wordsworth was to claim him for Aestheticism – to define him in terms of a literary stylist. To this end Pater begins his account by describing two quite separate qualities in Wordsworth's work, one of which he sees as possessing no value whatsoever, and the other which he praises very highly:

> For nowhere is there so perplexed a mixture as in Wordsworth's own poetry, of work touched with intense and individual power, with work of almost no character at all. He has much conventional sentiment, and some of that insincere poetic diction, against which his most serious critical efforts were directed: the reaction in his political ideas . . . makes him, at times, a mere declaimer on moral or social topics; and he seems, sometimes, to force an unwilling pen, and write by rule. By making the most of these blemishes it is possible to obscure the true aesthetic value of his work.[44]

Pater then goes onto define this 'aesthetic value' in terms identical to those used in the Preface to *The Renaissance*. Thus Wordsworth's literary 'power' becomes identified as the 'conveying to the consciousness of the reader, . . . impressions' which are realised through the employment of 'an absolute sincerity of feeling and diction'. His 'office', like that of all poets, 'is not [of] the moralist', but rather, 'to give the reader a peculiar kind of pleasure'. Like Leonardo and Browning before him, in Pater's hands Wordsworth becomes pre-eminently a stylist whose literariness resides in his attitude towards language:

> In regard to expression . . . it . . . was the pledge of its reality, to bring the appropriate language with it. In him, when the really poetical motive worked at all, it united, with absolute justice, the word and the idea. . . . His words are themselves thought and feeling; not eloquent, or musical words merely, but the sort of creative language which carries the reality of what it depicts, directly, to the consciousness.[45]

There are two points to notice here. The first concerns Pater's exploitation of an element common in Wordsworthian criticism. To advise reading Wordsworth with discrimination, acknowledging the coexistence of the very good and the very bad (in Pater's terms, the 'purely literary' and the 'alien' or non-literary) was not in itself unusual. So in 1869, for example, Arthur Clough had advised reducing Wordsworth's 'seven volumes to one',[46] a challenge later taken up by Arnold who recommended jettisoning 'the philosophy'. In suggesting that Wordsworth 'would gain most by a skilfully made anthology', Pater was thus keeping good company. However, the grounds upon which he proposed that such a selection be made were controversial for they virtually reversed all the usual oppositions. Thus, in Pater's eyes, to be 'conventional' (of 'sentiment', 'diction' or 'morals') was, by definition, to be 'insincere' and 'inexpressive' – and hence to be unliterary. To be unconventional, 'original' and 'individual', however, was to be 'serious', 'expressive' and thus highly literary. According to Pater, then, Wordsworth's work was actually marred by the same qualities which later critics, notably Arnold, would hold up as exemplary instances of 'genius'. Thus it is perhaps with a muted irony that Pater refers, in a footnote in the reprint of the essay in *Appreciations*, to 'selections [which] have been made [since this essay was written], with excellent taste, by Matthew Arnold'.[47] It is also worth noting that Pater's essay, 'Measure for Measure', published in 1874, the same year as the Wordsworth essay, and also reprinted in *Appreciations*, reinterpreted Shakespeare's work in a manner which challenged the later nationalist appropriations of him by critics such as Shairp and William Courthope. Although he noted the presence of many borrowings from contemporaries and predecessors in Shakespeare's work, Pater was mainly concerned to stress Shakespeare's uniqueness. He thus drew an important distinction between Whetstone's 'old story' (a contemporary source for *Measure for Measure*) and Shakespeare's play. The play, Pater argued, was marked off by its critical attitude towards 'the old "morality" ', towards the tendency of some early forms of drama to have 'for its function the inculcating of some moral theme'. In Pater's view the traces of this tendency which persisted in Shakespeare's play had been 'refashioned . . . in accordance with that artistic law which demands the predominance of form everywhere over the mere matter or subject handled', with the result that the 'ethical interest' in Whetstone's *Promos and Cassandra* became transformed in *Measure for Measure* to 'the [new] subject of poetical justice'. Pater goes on to define this quality in terms which by now appear familiar:

> Poetical justice . . . lies for the most part beyond the limits of any acknowledged law. The idea of justice involves the idea of rights. But at bottom rights are equivalent to that which really is, to facts; and the recognition of . . . rights therefore, . . . is the recognition of that which the person, in his inmost nature, really is. . . . It is . . . this finer justice, a justice based on a more delicate appreciation of the true conditions of men and things . . . which poetry cultivates in us the power of making [and] . . . which poetry actually requires.[48]

The second significant point in the essay on Wordsworth concerns Pater's placing of the poet within an established tradition; the qualities which he sees in Wordsworth are held to be 'exemplified, almost equally, by writers as unlike each other as Senancour and Théophile Gautier, . . . Rousseau, . . . Chateaubriand . . . [and] Hugo', as well as by painters such as Reynolds and Gainsborough.[49] Pater's redefinition of tradition is thus working at two levels. First it involves a self-conscious appropriation and reinterpretation of an eminent figure whose literary significance was a matter of contemporary debate or dispute. In this way the Wordsworth marginalised by orthodox literary judgements can have his reputation restored, and by resolving the difficulties of evaluating Wordsworth's poetry by emphasising his style, Pater is also able to draw attention to the limitations of usual definitions of literariness. Second, in order further to reinforce his claim about literariness, Pater invokes a new tradition, one already redefined in terms of stylistic originality. The combination of these two definitions – of an eminent figure and of a whole literary tradition – resulted in a strategy which Pater employed throughout his career. It is at work again, for example, in the essay on Charles Lamb. Lamb, too, is a singular stylist, marked off by the realisation in his prose of 'the principle of art for its own sake, . . . working ever close to the concrete, to the details, great or small, of actual things, books, persons'.[50] Pater's Lamb, 'delicate, refining, daintily epicurean' is, moreover, like Wordsworth, in a well-established tradition: this time the tradition of George Fox and particularly of Michel Montaigne; and 'Montaignesque' is the term Pater uses to describe 'that intimacy, that modern subjectivity'.

The most ambitious use of this strategy occurs in *Plato and Platonism*, Pater's last completed work. The importance of Plato to late nineteenth-century British literary culture hardly needs labouring. That Pater should chose to discuss Plato's writings at this point in his career is therefore wholly unremarkable; but the particular manner in which he used Plato as an authority for the practices of Aestheticism was anything but commonplace. *Plato and Platonism* marked itself off in several significant ways – in terms of content, methodology and so forth – from the main tradition of Platonic scholarship in the nineteenth century, particularly that of Jowett and his pupils. This process has been discussed comprehensively elsewhere,[51] and I am only concerned with one aspect of it – the attitude which Pater, as an aesthetic critic rather than historian of philosophy, adopted towards his subject, and the consequences of that attitude for his interpretation of Platonic ideas.

In the chapter entitled 'The Genius of Plato', Pater advocates what at first sight appears to be a conventional historicism, arguing that 'all true criticism . . . must begin with an historic estimate of the conditions, antecedent and contemporary, which helped make it precisely what it was.' He goes on to suggest that there is 'always also, as if acting from the opposite side, the comparatively inexplicable force of personality, resistant to, while it is moulded by, [circumstances].' It is this personality which is the proper subject for the critic:

> It might even be said that the trial-task of criticism, in regard to literature and art no less than to philosophy, begins exactly where the estimate of general conditions, of the conditions common to all the products of this or that particular age – of the 'environment' – leaves off, and we touch what is unique in the individual genius which contrived after all, by force of will, to have its own masterful way with that environment.[52]

Pater's examination of Plato's 'uniqueness' stresses his singular style: it is 'the special literary qualities' of the *Dialogues* rather than their moral or intellectual authority which commend them to Pater. He thus draws attention to the 'delightful aesthetic qualities' and 'figurative value' of Plato's vocabulary; and to the distinctiveness of his language, 'original, personal, the product of him'. The Plato of Pater, then, like his Leonardo, Dante and Wordsworth, is first and foremost 'a personality'; and Platonism is 'not a formal theory or body of theories, . . . but a tendency to think or feel, and to speak, about certain things in a particular way, discernible in Plato's dialogues as reflecting the peculiarities, the marked peculiarities, of himself and his own mental complexion.'[53] Moreover, throughout the book Pater invokes a lengthy catalogue of 'literary' figures who share the qualities of Plato's writing. In one chapter alone that catalogue includes figures as diverse as Sappho, Catullus, Charmides, Virgil, Milton, Raphael, Thackeray, Dante, Wordsworth and Tennyson.

Several critics, most notably Philip Appleman, have drawn attention to what they see as a profound contradiction between Pater's subjective and impressionistic aesthetic and his historicism; each of them, Appleman argues, 'to be consistent, requires the exclusion of the other'.[54] But in fact, as Pater's many examples make clear, there was in practice no real disjunction between the two positions. Whatever Pater meant by 'the historic sense' – and he never clearly defined the phrase – the implication of his appropriation of traditions for contemporary purposes was to demonstrate the constraints of historicism – to demonstrate, that is, that any account of the past was necessarily a construction placed upon it by the present. Such implications were not lost on Pater's contemporaries. Mrs Mark Pattison, for example, declared the 'History' of the original title of *The Renaissance* to be 'misleading', and 'the historical element [to be] precisely that which is wanting'.[55] Pater's adoption of two apparently contradictory positions was in fact a quite deliberate strategy, one which enabled him to negotiate the vexed problem produced by the intellectual conservatism of nineteenth-century Britain. It allowed him on the one hand to appear to recognise the authority of the past, and its role in shaping the present and future; and on the other, it gave him a freedom to reinterpret the past in such a way that it could be construed as the shaping force of his own (subversive) practices. Pater's insight was to recognise that although an age is formed by the traditions of its past, it also defines and redefines those traditions in terms appropriate to contemporary concerns. And his achievement was to exercise this prerogative in order to 'create' a 'constant tradition' of Aestheticism.

As I have argued in earlier chapters, French avant-gardes tend to oppose the past by proclaiming their newness or difference from it; Pater, on the other hand, paradoxically but understandably, given the British intellectual climate of the time, stressed the traditional nature of his practices. However, the difference between these two strategies is tactical rather than political. The main consequence in both cases was to undermine the orthodox view of tradition as a given of history. In the French example all traditions are rejected out of hand. In the British case it is the stability of tradition which is rejected. Pater's use of the past implied that traditions were inherently unstable, in need of constant reinterpretation by contemporary writers and artists in order to maintain a vitality and meaning.

Notes

1. Walter Pater, 'Shadwell's Dante' in *Uncollected Essays by Walter Pater* (Portland, Maine: Thomas B. Mosher, 1903), 145–61. Shadwell, fellow and later provost of Oriel College, was perhaps Pater's closest friend. *The Renaissance* was dedicated to him and he acted as Pater's literary executor.
2. During the second half of the nineteenth century there had been an intensification of interest in Dante culminating in the enormous proliferation of new translations which appeared in the 1880s and 1890s. Shadwell's contribution to this growth in Dante scholarship was an unusual one. Owing to the difficulties of rendering terza rima in English, most translators of Dante's work had used prose. Shadwell, however, attempted to get round this problem by using a quite different metrical pattern, that borrowed from Marvell's *Ode to Cromwell*. Contemporary critics were divided in their reactions to Shadwell's work. A more recent commentator, Gilbert Cunningham, has argued that 'it cannot be contended for a moment that Shadwell's stanzas convey any adequate notion of Dante's manner, even though they reproduce an amazing amount of his matter, and they would form a very poor guide for the reader whose knowledge of the Comedy can be obtained only from an English translation.' See Gilbert F. Cunningham, *The Divine Comedy in English: A Critical Bibliography 1782–1900* (London: Oliver and Boyd, 1965), 6–10, 179–86. Throughout the century there was also a great deal of disagreement over Dante's

significance. In the second half of the century these disagreements typically focused on the newly discovered 'Beatrice' of the *Vita Nuova*. Thus it was possible to find – on the one hand – Robert Buchanan's identification of Beatrice (and so too of Dante) with 'fleshliness' – 'the Italian disease'; and on the other, Theodore Martin's holding up the very same figure as sanctifying the highest ideal of Victorian womanhood. For an account of Dante's significance for the nineteenth century, see Steve Ellis, *Dante and English Poetry* (Cambridge: Cambridge, University Press, 1983).

3. Pater, 'Shadwell's Dante', 149.
4. Ibid. 147.
5. This connection has also been noted by Ian Small in 'Plato and Pater: Fin-de-Siècle Aesthetics', *British Journal of Aesthetics*, 12 (1972), 369–83.
6. Walter Pater, 'Style', *Appreciations* (London: Macmillan, 1913), 9–10.
7. Ibid. 12–15.
8. Ibid. 34.
9. Ibid. 22.
10. See Henry Mansel, *Prolegomena Logica* (Oxford: William Graham, 1851); and *The Philosophy of the Conditioned* (London: Alexander Strahan, 1866).
11. John Campbell Shairp, 'Aesthetic poetry: Dante Gabriel Rossetti', *Contemporary Review*, 42 (1882a), 22.
12. Unsigned review, 'The Poetry of Rossetti', *British Quarterly*, 76 (1882), 122.
13. Shairp, 'Aesthetic Poetry', 23.
14. John Campbell Shairp, 'English poets and Oxford critics', *Quarterly Review*, 153 (1882b), 442.
15. Walter Pater, *Marius the Epicurean*, ed. Ian Small (Oxford: Oxford University Press, 1986), 57.
16. Ibid. 55, 56.
17. Ibid. 58–9.
18. Ibid. 57–8.
19. Ibid. 57.
20. My understanding of Pater's attitudes towards tradition, particularly his interest in the Platonic idea of anamnesis, is indebted to a highly suggestive paper by William Shuter. See William F. Shuter, 'Pater's Reshuffled Text', *Nineteenth Century Literature*, 31 (1989), 500–25.
21. Carolyn Williams, 'Typology as narrative form: The temporal logic of *Marius*', *English Literature in Transition*, 27 (1984), 13.
22. See George P. Landow, *The Aesthetic and Critical Theories of John Ruskin* (Princeton, N.J.: Princeton University Press, 1971) and *William Holman Hunt and Typological Symbolism* (London: Yale University Press, 1979); see also Herbert L. Sussman, *Fact into Figure: Typology in Carlyle, Ruskin, and the Pre-Raphaelite Brotherhood* (Columbus, Ohio: Ohio University Press, 1979).
23. See Landow, *The Aesthetic and Critical Theories of John Ruskin*, 354 ff.

24. Northrop Frye, *The Great Code* (London: Routledge and Kegan Paul, 1982), 80–1.

25. See Linda Dowling, 'Roman decadence and Victorian historiography', *Victorian Studies*, 28 (1985), 579–607.

26. See Carolyn Williams, op. cit.; and Ian Small, Introduction to *Marius the Epicurean* (ed. cit.).

27. Although Carolyn Williams mentions in passing that Pater's 'literary use of typology is neither orthodox nor consistent throughout the text', she is nevertheless committed (by an argument which seeks to demonstrate that a typological reading of the novel can resolve 'some thorny problems and apparent contradictions') to assume that his use of the method is, broadly speaking, a conventional one.

28. Pater, 'Style', 9.

29. See Shuter, 506 ff.

30. Walter Pater, *The Renaissance*, ed. Donald Hill (Berkeley, Ca.: University of California Press, 1980), 76.

31. In *The Great Code* Frye also sees scriptural typology as similar to, and 'not impossibly connected with', Plato's view of knowledge as anamnesis. See 80 ff.

32. The description of the *Mona Lisa* is probably the most famous illustration of Pater's interest in anamnesis; Germain d'Hangest in *Walter Pater: L'homme et l'oeuvre* (Paris: Didier, 1961) has argued that Pater's whole conception of the Renaissance is based upon Platonic ideas of pre-existence. Pater's use of the idea of prefigurement can, however, be traced back further: as William Shuter has demonstrated, it first appears in 'Diaphaneitè', written in 1864. See Shuter, op. cit., 512.

33. Walter Pater, *Plato and Platonism* (London: Macmillan, 1893), 2–3.

34. Ibid. 3–4. In this respect it is worth noting Edmund Gosse's view of tradition in his *A Short History of English Literature* (London: Heinemann, 1898):

> What we are in the habit of describing as 'originality' in a great modern poet is largely an aggregation of elements which he has received by inheritance from those who have preceded him, and his 'genius' consists of the faculty he possesses of selecting and rearranging, as in a new pattern of harmony, those elements from many predecessors which most admirably suit the only 'new' thing about him, his unique set of personal characteristics. (391–2)

35. See in particular William Shuter, op. cit., and Ian Small, Introduction to *Marius the Epicurean*.

36. Walter Pater, *The Renaissance*, ed. cit., 78.

37. Ibid. 92.

38. Ibid. 93–7.

39. Ibid. 95.

40. John Stuart Mill, *Autobiography, Collected Works of John Stuart Mill*, I, eds. John M. Robson and Jack Stillinger (London: University of Toronto Press, 1981b), 153.

41. See Matthew Arnold, 'Wordsworth', *Macmillan's Magazine*, 40 (1879a),

103–204. The essay was also printed in *Poems of Wordsworth* (London: Macmillan, 1879b).

42. Arnold, 'Wordsworth', *Macmillan's Magazine*, 199–201.
43. For example, for Shairp 'Wordsworth's obscurest sonnet [was] . . . transparent compared with even the average of Rossetti's.' See Shairp, 'Aesthetic poetry', 29.
44. Pater, 'Wordsworth', *Appreciations*, 40.
45. Ibid. 57–8.
46. Arthur Hugh Clough, *Poems and Prose Remains* (London: Macmillan, 1869), 318.
47. Pater, 'Wordsworth', 43.
48. Pater, 'Measure for Measure', *Appreciations*, 182–4.
49. Pater, 'Wordsworth', 43–4.
50. Walter Pater, 'Charles Lamb' *Appreciations*, 109. The essay was originally published in the *Fortnightly Review* in October 1878.
51. For a general discussion of the relationship between *Plato and Platonism* and contemporary scholarship see Ian Small, 'Plato and Pater: Fin-de-Siècle Aesthetics', op. cit.
52. Pater, *Plato and Platonism*, 112.
53. Ibid. 136.
54. See Philip Appleman, 'Darwin and Pater's Critical Dilemma', *Darwin: A Norton critical edition*, ed. Philip Appleman (New York: Norton, 1970).
55. Mrs Mark Pattison, 'Art', *Westminster Review*, 43 (1873), 639.

CHAPTER 6

William Morris:
Tradition and revolution

At first glance the term avant-garde might appear to be a more appropriate description of William Morris than of a writer such as Pater. Indeed, as I have indicated, Donald Drew Egbert, one of the few historians of avant-gardism to take account of nineteenth-century Britain, sees Morris as a dominant figure.[1] However, it is significant that Morris is included in Egbert's history solely on the grounds of his political radicalism; it is Morris's role in the development of British socialism, rather than his career as a writer or painter, which has enabled him to be described as avant-garde.

The reason for the marginalisation of Morris the writer is that in a miniature, as it were, of the main problem of British avant-gardism; namely, that the relationship between politics and aesthetics in his work is a vexed one: there appears to be a profound contradiction between his socialism, his view of revolutionary social change, and the dependence of his literary works upon tradition, both in terms of their form and their subject. This contradiction is most keenly felt in the opposition between Morris's demands, made most forcefully in his lectures, for a popular art form – *'an art which is to be made by the people and for the people'*[2] – and the exclusive, even undemocratic nature of the styles he employed in his own work. Morris's use of Icelandic sagas, verbal archaisms (such as the use of the 'thou' and the verbal form *-eth* for the second person singular in *News from Nowhere*) and medieval narrative techniques (as in *The Dream of John Ball*) made his writing 'difficult', and like Pater and Rossetti, he was accused of obscurity and affectation.[3] Morris's reluctance to embrace popular contemporary forms and his hostility towards the formal innovations of other avant-gardes thus give him the appearance of being deeply conservative, a position which consorts strangely with his socialist politics. As Egbert comments, 'in many respects he was far from being avant-garde . . . . [He] could not accept the work of artistically progressive artists and writers who, like him, were concerned with social problems.'[4]

The apparent discrepancy between Morris's radical political views and the traditionalism of his literary works has often been noted, but rarely explained adequately.[5] Most accounts of Morris's radicalism have tended simply to marginalise his literary works. So for critics such as Raymond Williams, E. P. Thompson – and, more recently, even Paul Meier – Morris's radicalism is seen principally (if not solely) in his activities in organisations such as the Socialist League and in his political pamphlets and lectures written during the 1870s, 1880s and 1890s. As they define these terms, Morris the 'political' radical is effectively bracketed off from Morris the literary artist.[6] The limitations of these kinds of accounts of Morris's radicalism are two-fold. In general terms, as John Goode has suggested, there is a problem of 'value'. Since one of the distinguishing features of Morris's socialism is the social role he grants to art, it is important that Morris's own literary work should be seen fulfilling that function. To reject his creative writing is 'to call into question the whole social criticism – it relies too much on what seems to be a bad conception of art'.[7] The second and related problem is one specific to avant-garde histories. In the terms of these histories, Morris clearly cannot be accommodated within a tradition of cultural avant-gardism for his literary work is simply not oppositional in nature – not, that is, in the senses in which opposition is usually defined.[8] In order to make a case for Morris to be seen as an avant-garde figure it is important to explain the radical political views advocated in his lectures and the traditionalist aesthetic of his literary works within the same frame of reference; the latter, as Goode suggests, has to be seen in some way as an appropriate response to the former. Two observations, about Morris's socialism and about his literary works, suggest the direction in which this task might proceed.

In the first place, it is striking that in all Morris's writing – in his lectures, pamphlets, literary works, and so on – there is no detailed and convincing explanation of the process or means of revolutionary change. Tireless in pointing out ills in contemporary society, and equally insistent in pressing his vision of the socialist future, for a 'revolutionary' Morris seemed remarkably vague about the question of how precisely social change is to come about. It is this larger issue, rather than simply that of Morris's ability to provide a convincing account of the function of art in the revolutionary process, which needs to be explained. It suggests that the so-called 'weakness' of Morris's aesthetic – in Thompson's words, Morris's failure 'to construct a theory [of art] both consistent with a materialist conception of history, and adequate to explain the active part of the artist in the ideological struggles of his time'[9] – might in fact be a characteristic of his socialism in general. If this is so, then an explanation of this latter, more general weakness may provide an answer to the problem of his role as a radical literary artist.

In the second place, it is equally striking that the work of other (particularly French) avant-garde writers who held equally radical political views is not marked with the same contradictions. In this respect, an illuminating comparison can be made between Morris and Courbet. Morris's proposals for a popular art-form have some parallels with Courbet's ambition to create 'l'art démocratique'. Both Morris and Courbet were conspicuous in proclaiming their solidarity with 'le peuple' and both claimed to be opposed to all forms of élitism, especially those associated with the institutions of art. Both also held radical political views. Morris's were indebted to a number of figures, the most important of which were Cobbett, Owen, Kropotkin and Marx; and Courbet's derived from his experience of revolution, and from the writing of Henri de Saint-Simon and his friendship with the anarchist Proudhon. However, the similarities between these two figures end when we consider the relationship between their declared political ambitions for art and the actual works which they produced. Unlike Morris, who used traditional forms and subjects, Courbet attempted to develop an art appropriate to a revolutionary climate and deliberately broke from artistic traditions. The democratisation of art required new forms and new subjects; and in Courbet's Realist paintings it is the people, rather than eminent historical figures or historical events, which become the subjects. Moreover they were depicted in ways indebted to popular, contemporary iconography rather than the idealising forms of the Academy. The question suggested by this comparison is why did Courbet, but not Morris, see the rejection of artistic traditions as both appropriate and realisable in the development of a revolutionary iconography and symbolism?

The explanation of the singularity of Morris's position lies in factors unique to British culture. Both the general question of Morris's politics – his apparent difficulty in envisaging the precise ways in which a revolution might take place in contemporary Britain – and the more specific question of his use of traditional forms and subjects in his literary works can be explained in terms of the profound intellectual conservatism which I have suggested characterised nineteenth-century Britain. That conservatism operated upon Morris in two related ways. In a general sense, it conditioned the nature of his socialist polemic; as I shall indicate, it determined his use of certain apparently 'conservative' concepts – in particular, his holding to an attenuated notion of historical continuity and his appreciation of the important role played by traditions in contemporary society. However, that intellectual conservatism also put limits on Morris's aesthetic or formal choices; it constrained them to borrowing of traditional literary forms and subjects rather than to the invention of new ones, for in Britain such a strategy was an entirely appropriate (and even necessary) response to the task of 'revolutionising' contemporary literature.

The concept of revolutionary social change, as I have indicated, was foreign to nineteenth-century British culture. It is significant that even in the 1870s, when attitudes towards the past had become problematised, the main theory of social change to emerge in Britain, that of Spencerian sociology, was evolutionary rather than revolutionary in character. It should not seem surprising, then, that having enthusiastically embraced the revolutionary politics of socialism in the intellectual ferment of the late 1870s, Morris subsequently encountered considerable difficulties in applying them to the British context. Whatever the appeal of socialism – and the possibility of a wholly new social order was clearly an attractive answer to Morris's long standing discontent with contemporary society – in Britain there was simply no intellectual tradition to support a theory of radical social change. Morris's growing realisation of the practical difficulties involved in bringing about a socialist revolution in Britain – the problem, that is, of an appropriate form of political action – has often been noticed. The early revolutionary optimism which led to his disagreements with Hyndman, and his subsequent break from the Social Democratic Federation over the issue of 'state socialism' in the 1870s, was gradually replaced by more sober reflection on the diminishing possibility of the revolution – evidence perhaps that, along with his disillusionment, Morris had developed a certain political 'pragmatism'. Less frequently noted than these practical political difficulties, however, is Morris's acute awareness of the intellectual constraints imposed by the uniqueness of the British intellectual climate – of the inappropriateness of applying certain kinds of political ideas in relation to British history. He frequently commented, for example, on the hostility aroused by the term 'revolution', attributing much of the misunderstanding which greeted British socialism to its association with the destructive lawlessness of the Jacobinism of the French.

> The word Revolution, which we Socialists are so often forced to use, has a terrible sound in most people's ears, even when we have explained to them that it does not necessarily mean a change accompanied by riot and all kinds of violence, and cannot mean a change made mechanically and in the teeth of opinion by a group of men who have some how managed to seize on the executive power for the moment. Even when we explain that we use the word revolution in its etymological sense, and we mean by it a change in the basis of society, people are scared at the idea of such vast change, and beg that you will speak of reform and not revolution.[10]

Like others adopting new ideas in late nineteenth-century Britain, Morris was forced to adapt the revolutionary concepts of socialism to meet the demands of British *intellectual* (rather than simply political) conservatism. Indeed he used the term 'reconstructive Socialism' to replace 'revolution'.[11] He had to find a way of reconciling two opposing views of the past – the concept of radical social change, common to French revolutionary historiography, and the concept of constitutional continuity held by most British historians. At an intellectual level, then, the issue facing Morris was identical with the one which faced all avant-garde artists and writers in Britain. In attempting to introduce revolutionary socialism into Britain, and to create a revolutionary art-form, Morris had to negotiate a new relationship with the past, a task rendered peculiarly problematic in Britain by the difficulties involved in the direct repudiation of traditions. Moreover, Morris's response to this historiographical impasse was equally in keeping with the solutions found by other British avant-garde writers. In Morris's eyes, the intellectual bridge between the revolutionary and evolutionary views of historical change was supplied by a third concept, that of tradition: traditions bore witness to the continuity of history – they were, as most British historians recognised, an important record of human endeavours and aspirations; but at the same time they were also the enabling condition for radical change. What precisely Morris meant by this paradox is best illustrated by a comparison with his immediate predecessors, the Pre-Raphaelite Brotherhood, of which he was at one time a member, and with his contemporaries, the Aesthetes. First, however, it is useful to examine further the nature of the intellectual problem he faced, and a useful means of doing so is provided by his defence of his activities with 'Antiscrape', set out in a series of papers delivered to the Society for the Protection of Ancient Buildings (SPAB) in the late 1870s and 1880s.

The society was founded by Morris in the 1870s in reaction to a current fashion for 'restoring' ancient buildings in imitation of the Gothic style. Morris justified his campaigning against this practice in terms of a need to avoid attempted reproductions of the past. He argued that buildings should be 'preserved' rather than restored – that is, that basic structural repairs and so forth should be made where necessary, but that there should be no attempt to impose a particular style on a building, as with, for example, the tendency to 'correct' later additions by replacing them with imitations of some notional – generally Gothic – 'original' style. Moreover, he maintained that the distinctiveness of preservation, as opposed to restoration, was that it did not imply that art of the past should or could be imitated; on the contrary. The historical uniqueness of the conditions under which such art was produced explicitly precluded such a possibility. Underlying Morris's views was a belief in the importance of tradition in contemporary society; the protection of ancient buildings was necessary, according to Morris, because those buildings, like all artefacts, embodied the unique values of the particular culture which had produced them, and so represented an important historical record, one which could be destroyed by unsympathetic hands.

The especial value to which I wish to-day to call your attention [is that] . . . ancient architecture bears witness to the development of man's ideas, to the continuity of history, and, so doing, affords never-ceasing instruction, nay education, to the passing generations, not only telling us what were the aspirations of men passed away, but also what we may hope for in time to come.[12]

This argument is in fact very close to the claims about tradition made by conservative figures such as William Courthope; it appears to invoke the same historiographical assumptions used by the proponents of a national literature. Indeed that same year, in the context of a different lecture, Morris had defined as one of the necessary prerequisites for a 'decent life' an 'active mind in sympathy with the past'.[13] Stated in terms as general as these, contemporaries such as Courthope certainly would not have disagreed with such an ambition. What then distinguished Morris's views of the past and what made them appear subversive? A clue is provided in a later paper, delivered to the SPAB in 1889; here Morris argued his position more carefully, drawing attention to the difference between his understanding of the concept of 'historical continuity' and that used by his contemporaries:

> I say that the straining of the ideas of the continuity of history – although there is a certain interest in it – is now pedantry; not wholly dull and stupid pedantry, but founded on a misconception. . . . Persons with that false idea of the continuity of history are loath to admit the fatal words, 'it cannot be, it has gone'. They believe that we can do the same sort of work in the same spirit as our forefathers, whereas for good and for evil we are completely changed, and we cannot do the work they did. All continuity of history means is after all perpetual change, and it is not hard to see that we have changed with a vengeance, and thereby established our claim to be the continuers of a nation.[14]

Clearly, as critics such as E. P. Thompson have been keen to point out, Morris is far from exhibiting the 'conservatism' which his campaigning on behalf of the protection of ancient buildings might suggest: he is no 'nostalgic' revivalist or 'sentimental pedant'.[15] At the same time, however, there is an important sense in which Morris appears reluctant to reject completely those very orthodoxies about the past which Thompson wants to distance him from. Rather than dismiss altogether the concept of historical continuity, Morris instead attempts elaborately, and somewhat confusingly, to redefine it – to accommodate it within a concept of social change. That he attempts such an accommodation (or feels the need to do so) is evidence of the difficulties involved in replacing wholesale current intellectual orthodoxies in Britain with new or foreign ideas. Morris's attitude towards the past was, then, determined by a characteristically British paradox: an awareness of two contradictory impulses, the first being that traditions had a 'negative and conservative power [which] . . . keeps people from changing the general tendency of . . . Art [or society]',[16] and the second that a culture was simply 'not able to dispense with tradition'.[17] It was, in other words, exactly the problem which faced all nineteenth-century avant-garde figures, including Pater and Wilde, who were, to borrow Peter Faulkner's phrase, 'against the age': it was the problem of the vexed relationship between the radical or innovative individual and the pervasive authority of tradition.

The suggestion that there are analogies between Morris's and Pater's position may seem a perverse one. Indeed most accounts of Morris's radicalism have tended to define it against his literary and artistic contemporaries and predecessors: against, on the one hand, the 'idealism' and 'political naivety' of the Pre-Raphaelite Brotherhood (Morris's association with the Brotherhood is dismissed by Thompson as mere 'youthful revolt'); and, on the other, the alleged conservatism and apolitical stance of the Aesthetes. As I have indicated, an examination of the relationships between Morris and these two groups sheds further light on his attitudes towards the past and tradition.

It has been argued that Morris's career underwent a decisive turning point around 1877, the moment when he first entered public politics over the Eastern question, first came in contact with socialism, delivered his first overtly political lecture and began to distance himself from Pre-Raphaelite ideas. This last move is described in terms of Morris's rejection of the Brotherhood's allegedly 'escapist' idealisation of the past and his development instead of a more 'serious', more critical perspective, one which was aware of historical process and aware too of the inevitability of social change. In this view Morris's intellectual break from Pre-Raphaelitism becomes one of the keys to understanding his new political awareness: Morris 'the revolutionary' begins, it is argued, at the point where the Pre-Raphaelite idealist ends.[18]

The suggestion that Morris departed from Pre-Raphaelite ideals is, however, misleading, for it is based on a misunderstanding of the subversive nature of the Brotherhood's use of tradition. Indeed Morris himself never acknowledged such a rupture. His address, 'The English Pre-Raphaelites', delivered in 1891 on the occasion of an exhibition of the Brotherhood's work at the Birmingham Museum and Art Gallery, was a tribute to the movement's achievements, both aesthetic *and* political. Morris gave a particular emphasis, for example, to the serious nature of the Pre-Raphaelite revolt: 'these few young men', he argued, 'wholly unknown till they *forced* the public to recognise them, began what must be called a really audacious attempt; a definite revolt against the Academical Art which brooded over all the Schools of Europe at the time.'[19] Morris's argument is that the main impetus behind the formation of the Brotherhood was a growing impatience with the Academy's conventionalism. Frustrated by its tendency to encourage imitations of established styles rather than the development of new ones, and resentful of the authority embodied in the example of Joshua Reynolds, Rossetti, Holman Hunt, Millais and Woolner founded the Pre-Raphaelite Brotherhood to reinvigorate British art. Such a view was confirmed by that of the Brotherhood's first historian, William Michael Rossetti. William Rossetti had suggested that the Brotherhood had two principal aims: one was to encourage artists 'to develop their own individuality, disregarding school-rules';[20] and the other was to restore an 'authentic' tradition of Western pictorial art by locating its birth in medieval Italian painting.

At first glance, such aims may appear contradictory: the desire to encourage innovation and individuality does not square easily with the notion of a perpetuating tradition. However, the concept of tradition which the Brotherhood had in mind was a different one from that held by the Academy. In proposing early Italian artists as their models, the Brotherhood did not simply replace one set of idols – the Old Masters – with another; rather they argued that the exemplary nature of artists such as Giotto, Masaccio and Gozzoli lay not in their style, but an attitude which they took towards their subject matter. The Brotherhood further claimed that this attitude – 'an entire adherence to the simplicity of nature'[21] – was the basic precondition for innovation in art. By emulating early Italian models the modern painter, according to the Brotherhood, was merely reproducing the conditions necessary for the expression of individuality. In the Pre-Raphaelite manifesto, *The Germ*, F. G. Stephens had described the Brotherhood's attempt 'to lead the taste of the public into a new channel by producing pure transcripts and faithful studies from nature, instead of conventionalities and feeble reminiscences from Old Masters.' He went on to explain that this tactic entailed 'an entire seeking after originality in a more humble manner than has been practised since the decline of Italian Art in the Middle Ages.'[22]

By seeing a tradition as the embodiment of the preconditions which made 'authentic' art possible, rather than as the exemplification of a particular style, the Brotherhood claimed, without any sense of a contradiction, to be both endorsing originality and respecting a tradition.

That the Brotherhood saw themselves as innovators rather than mere revivalists has tended to have been ignored, both by nineteenth- and twentieth-century critics. However, the Brotherhood were explicit about their intentions; in his retrospective account of the movement, William Holman Hunt took this issue up. Hunt described the Brotherhood's 'sympathy' with the work of Gozzoli, and the subsequent decision to make him 'the standard under which we were to make our advance', but he stressed that such a view did not entail an uncritical imitation of his style:

> We did not curb our amusement at the immature perspective, the undeveloped power of drawing, the feebleness of light and shade, the ignorance of any but the mere black and white differences of racial types of men, the stinted variety of flora, and their geometrical forms in the landscape; these simplicities, already out of date in the painter's day, we noted as belonging altogether to the past and to the dead revivalists, with whom we had determined to have neither part nor lot. . . . The assumption that all our circle knew [was] that deeper devotion to Nature's teaching was the real point at which we were aiming.[23]

There is ample evidence to suggest that Hunt's account of the Brotherhood's activities was not one shared by contemporary critics. One of their fiercest critics, the reviewer for *The Times*, for example, was typical in claiming that 'these young artists have unfortunately become notorious by addicting themselves to an antiquated style and an affected simplicity in Painting, which is to genuine art what the medieval ballads and designs in *Punch* are to Chaucer and Giotto.'[24] The fortunes of the Brotherhood, mixed as they were, relate to the enduring power of British orthodoxies, especially in the mid-nineteenth century, to assimilate and marginalise forms of dissent. Nevertheless the mixed nature of their success should not be allowed to obscure the fact that in its initial conception, the Brotherhood's revolt was 'intended' to be revolutionary. Indeed William Michael Rossetti described the Brotherhood as having 'meant revolt and produced revolution'.[25] It was precisely this 'intention' – an ambition to use the past or tradition only in order to 'create something new' – which Morris recognised as marking the uniqueness of the Brotherhood's achievement, and which he acknowledged in his address as the only viable strategy for the innovative artist or writer in Britain.

> I say by all means let us cultivate whatever there may be left of any wish to get back into the best traditions of Art. Those traditions we must undoubtedly work up again for ourselves. They must help us to produce something which has not been produced before. We cannot do the work of the past again. We don't want it, and it would be no particular use if we could; but whether we want it or not it is absolutely certain that we cannot do it.[26]

These words echo a much earlier comment in 1877 on ancient art: 'let us therefore study it wisely, be taught by it, kindled by it; all the while determining not to imitate or repeat it'.[27] What did Morris mean by this injunction? In what sense was knowledge of the past 'useful' if traditions could not be repeated? It is clear that Morris is advocating a quite different view of tradition from that held by the majority of his contemporaries; in his eyes, traditions did not and could not have a normative function. Secondly, it is equally clear that Morris did not mean the injunction to be a purely negative one. Earlier in the same lecture he had suggested the positive application which knowledge of traditions might have: '[for] those . . . [who] can do nothing else', he argued, 'it may be their business to keep alive some tradition, some memory of the past, so that the new life when it comes may not waste itself more than enough in fashioning wholly new forms for its new spirit.'[28] Morris seems to suggest that tradition could in some way provide models which, reworked, or – to borrow Pater's term – 'rehabilitated' might form the basis of the new society, or indeed of a new art. Moreover, in so far as that new society would have its origins (however attenuated) in those old models or traditions, so they would come to be authorised by them. As Pater had recognised, the new was, in an important sense, the old also; hence Morris's dictum that 'all continuity of history means is after all perpetual change'.

Morris systematically worked up or reinterpreted certain aspects of the medieval past in order to authorise his socialist politics, in order to create, to use Pater's terms again, a 'constant tradition' of socialism. The extent (though not the significance) of this interpretation has been scrupulously documented by Margaret Grennan.[29] She highlights four general areas where the partiality of that interpretation is particularly striking. The first and most 'innocent' concerns his idealised treatment of medieval craftsmen. As Grennan points out, although scholarship since Morris's day has heavily qualified his view, in the nineteenth century the 'miracle' of the organisation of labour required by Gothic architecture demanded explanation, and that supplied by Morris had been endorsed by Ruskin in *The Stones of Venice* and thus seemed plausible. The second and more self-consciously propagandist area concerns Morris's attempt to revalue the hierarchical political structures of feudalism. Unlike conservatives such as Carlyle, who had seen in feudal society an admirable form of authoritarianism, Morris pointed to the existence of an important, if frequently imperfectly executed, principle of 'rights and personal duties'. It was the existence of this principle, largely free from hypocrisy, which, according to Morris, made medieval society, for all its manifest inequalities, preferable to the contract based society of contemporary capitalism. The third area where Morris's partiality is exhibited concerns his profound underestimate of the importance of the medieval Catholic Church, particularly with regard to the roles played by religious mysticism and piety. Significantly, the one positive function which Morris did attribute to the Church was its success in fostering what he claimed was a genuinely corporate spirit. The fourth and most important area of Morris's rewriting concerns his attention to the medieval guilds. In Morris's eyes they epitomised the communal and democratic spirit characteristic of socialist society; they foreshadowed 'the pleasure of life [which] might be in a society of equals'.[30] But it is interesting to notice, as Grennan points out, that contemporary medieval scholarship, of which Morris was certainly well aware, had presented a very different picture of guild life, one characterised by rivalry, self-interest and an exclusivity which, according to some historians, was the principal cause of the guilds' demise.

In one sense this overtly propagandist rewriting of medievalism was not particularly new. As Charles Dellheim suggests, medievalism was not the exclusive cultural property of conservatives; it had also been appropriated by early nineteenth-century radicals, most significantly by William Cobbett in his *A History of the Protestant Reformation in England and Ireland* (1824), to endorse arguments for political and social democracy.[31] However, by the time Morris was writing, historiography had greatly changed. The better availability of sources and the Rankean emphasis on facts, which I have described, had made both the deliberate manipulations of Cobbett's history on the one hand, and the dramatic and personal style of Carlyle's *Past and Present* on the other, unacceptable. Much more representative of late nineteenth-century medieval historiography was the work of Edward Freeman. A Tory turned Liberal, and one of the chief campaigners for the professionalisation of the discipline of history, Freeman used medievalism to trace a tradition of English liberty which authorised liberal programmes for political reform. It is against the work of figures such as Freeman that Morris's medievalism should thus be seen. In this respect two points are important. First, Morris's use of the medieval past to authorise a revolutionary socialist, rather than reformist liberal, political tradition was highly unorthodox; secondly, that his methods of so doing were quite different from those of historians; as Grennan indicates, Morris presented a 'generalized picture' – a 'delineation of the past in broad strokes rather than the penetrating criticism of particular phases of life or thought'.[32]

Morris was clearly not in competition with historians; the much stricter methodological paradigms characteristic of late nineteenth-century historiography made a straightforwardly historical account of the medieval past in terms of a socialist tradition both implausible and very difficult to execute. In this respect Morris's selective use of historical sources, his refusal to engage with contemporary debates in historiography about the significance of certain aspects of medievalism, and his cavalier disregard for the scholarship which controverted his political thesis, is illuminating. Morris's reworking of medievalism was quite deliberately an imaginative rather than a scholarly one. Drawing upon literary qualities, its appeal was emotional and dramatic rather than intellectual. In this sense the significance of the prose romances for Morris's overall political ambitions can easily be seen. Literary forms, especially those of dream and vision, themselves borrowed from medieval literature, gave Morris a much greater licence to rework history than the scholarly rhetoric of historiography; they enabled him, that is, to ground the apparently 'unreal' – those revolutionary concepts and ideas which were foreign to Britain – in what the general reader, familiar with the themes and tropes of medievalism but not necessarily with debates in medieval historical scholarship, would recognise as a framework of historical fact. The dream of revolution in, say, *The Dream of John Ball* or *News From Nowhere*, becomes 'real' (and therefore convincing) precisely to the extent that it can be seen to have a basis in 'real' historical events. Other formal qualities of Morris's literary works, in particular his use of linguistic archaisms in order to recreate an 'authentic' medieval voice, can also be seen as part of this self-consciously literary, as opposed to historiographical, reworking of medievalism. The use of 'thou', and of archaisms such as 'betwixt' and 'forsooth', were part of Morris's general attempt to realise the medieval past in a manner not open to historians. In ways such as these the specifically literary artifices of the prose romance made 'conceivable' (and therefore possible) those revolutionary concepts which orthodox historiography had largely rejected.[33] 'What romance means', Morris argued, 'is the capacity for a true conception of history, a power of making the past part of the present.'[34]

It is not surprising, then, to find that Morris takes much greater liberties with historical evidence in his literary works than in his lectures or pamphlets. In the *The Dream of John Ball*, for example, Morris rewrites his historical sources – those concerning the Peasants' Revolt of 1381 on which the narrative is based – in several significant ways. First, and most importantly, he presents a totally erroneous thesis concerning the cause and effect of the revolt. This major error has often been explained in terms of Morris's dependence upon Thorold Rogers, whose thesis on the causes of the revolt, despite its unsupportable generalisations, had attained the status of an orthodoxy between the late 1860s and the early 1890s, when it was discredited by the work of historians such as André Reville and Charles Oman. In view of his own detailed reading of many of Rogers's sources, it is unlikely that Morris was unaware of the obvious flaws in the thesis. In fact Morris, like Rogers, greatly romanticises the revolt: he underplays its violence and exaggerates the open nature of the contest; he moves the action from London to the country; he 'invents' a battle (there were no encounters between the peasants and troops of the kind Morris describes) and conjures up a sermon, the dramatic centrepiece of the narrative, for which there is no historical counterpart; and he significantly reorders the chronology. Morris also takes liberties with historical characters, unjustifiably attributing 'communist' motives both to his protagonist, John Ball, and to the rebel peasants. Grennan argues that there is virtually no evidence in the chronicles to support such an interpretation, and quotes Trevelyan's opinion that 'the attempt to picture the rising as a communistic movement ignores the plainest facts'. She goes on to describe Morris having 'deliberately in some cases . . . ignored the scope, [and] the complexity . . . of the rising and once at least, . . . [having] read more into the sources than the record will justify'.[35] But of course for the literary artist, rather than the historian, all these 'liberties' are perfectly justified: historical accuracy can be sacrificed for dramatic or literary purposes. Similar strategic rewritings can be found in Morris's other prose romances. *The House of the Wolfings*, for example, is also based upon a 'core of historical reality', the most significant aspect of which is the 'mark', the name given to a primitive form of communal village life in Germany. In Morris's narrative the German mark, like the Peasants' Revolt, becomes a site of early communist associations, represented by a detailed description of the Wolfing's homelife and a dramatic account of the battle against the invading Romans. However, at the time when Morris was working, contemporary historical scholarship was undecided about the nature and significance of the mark. An influential group of historians, headed by the Frenchman, Fustel de Coulanges, had challenged the 'Teutonic' tradition of scholarship which Morris had drawn upon, arguing that the premiss that English liberties (however defined) could be traced back to an ideal of fellowship embodied in the German mark was erroneous. Morris, however, appears to have ignored the whole 'Romanist' critique, exaggerating instead the very elements of Teutonism which that critique had disputed.

The 'success' of Morris's literary works – in John Goode's terms, the extent to which they are able to make revolutionary concepts 'conceivable' – depends upon the balance struck between the fictional or literary elements and the framework of historical 'fact'. In many of the later prose romances, such as *Child Christopher and Goldilind the Fair* (1895) and *The Well at the World's End* (1896), the literary overwhelms the historical as Morris's borrowings from the past become increasingly eclectic. The consequence, of course, is that the political propaganda becomes correspondingly less 'real' and the concept of revolution becomes grounded in myth rather than history. One reason for this may simply be Morris's growing disillusionment; as the prospect of a socialist revolution in Britain receded, so Morris's representations of revolution swerve further away from any recognisable historical 'facts'.[36] In this sense, certain of the later prose romances may justifiably be accused of a romantic idealism. However, to concede this point is only to suggest that Morris's earlier literary works are more successful than his later ones, and that these successes coincide, not unreasonably, with the height of his enthusiasm and confidence in the revolutionary cause.

In general terms, then, Morris used medievalism to authorise his socialist politics; revolution became possible or conceivable in Britain to the extent that it could be seen to possess a historical precedent, one which, by being located in the English past, was significantly different to that so feared in France. It is in this sense, then, that traditions can be seen to have provided the enabling condition for social change in Britain – they presented social change as a real possibility – and that Morris's literary art can be seen as a genuine attempt to create a revolutionary art form, one entirely appropriate to his socialist politics. Moreover, it is in this 'positive' use of tradition to 'create something new', that Morris was substantially indebted to his Pre-Raphaelite colleagues. His use of tradition was certainly more complex than theirs; the suggestion that traditions had a 'negative' as well as 'positive' role added an ambiguity absent from the Brotherhood's interest in medieval Italian art. Absent, too, from their interest was Morris's use of tradition for overtly party-political ends. However, in his basic recognition that contemporary orthodoxies could be overturned in Britain only through the reworking of traditions, Morris was at one both with the Brotherhood and, more importantly, with the Aesthetes.

The suggestion that Morris had certain strategic affinities with the Aesthetes, and that his avant-gardism can be understood in the same terms as theirs is novel and so needs some qualification. At one level Morris's politics were clearly very different from those of Aestheticism. He attacked the doctrine of 'art for art's sake' on numerous occasions, objecting to its élitism and its attempt to remove art from a social domain:

> I do not want art for a few, any more than that education for a few, or freedom for a few. No, rather than art should live this poor thin life among a few exceptional men, despising those beneath them for an ignorance for which they themselves are responsible, for a brutality that they will not struggle with, – rather than this, I would that the world should indeed sweep away all art for awhile . . . . Rather than the wheat should rot in the miser's granary, I would that the earth had it, that it might yet have a chance to quicken in the dark.[37]

Despite holding quite different views from the Aesthetes on the nature and function of art, Morris nevertheless shared with them one fundamental characteristic. The strategy which he adopted to articulate his views – the use of tradition to challenge contemporary orthodoxies and thus to underwrite his politics – was exactly the same as that which the Aesthetes employed. He shared their recognition that 'revolutionaries' in Britain had to accommodate themselves to tradition. There were, of course, other less welcome similarities with the Aesthetes. The ornate and archaic language of some of Morris's poetry and prose romances, and the elaborate publications of the Kelmscott Press (they were described by one critic as 'printed for the aesthetic few'[38]) laid him open to exactly the allegations of obscurantism, artifice and élitism which accompanied the works of Aestheticism. Also, in light of Morris's own prescriptions for a popular art form, one 'by the people and for the people', they were much more difficult to counter. Indeed, this particular affinity was not lost on the Aesthetes: Morris was, for example, the subject of a review by Pater, the last paragraphs of which later became the famous 'Conclusion' to *The Renaissance*; Wilde also appropriated him, playfully referring in 'The English Renaissance of Art' to Morris's 'faultless devotion to beauty'.[39]

It is only by placing Morris's literary art in its unique *intellectual* (rather than social or political) context that its radicalism can properly be assessed and the contradictions between Morris's aesthetics and politics explained. In particular, such a context allows Morris's art to be seen as an entirely appropriate, if not always completely successful, response to his political vision. In his use of the past – his appropriation of a medieval tradition in order to provide context, form and rationale for his radical politics – Morris was merely exhibiting a characteristic which was common to all avant-garde writers and artists in Britain, including acknowledged adversaries such as Whistler. The uniqueness of Morris lies only in the consequences of that attempt to accommodate himself to tradition.

Notes

1. See Donald Drew Egbert, *Social Radicalism and the Western Arts: Western Europe* (London: Duckworth, 1970), 424 ff.

2. William Morris, 'The art of the people', *The Collected Works of William Morris*, ed. May Morris (London: Longman, 1910–15), XXII, 47.
3. See Peter Faulkner (ed.), *William Morris: The critical heritage* (London: Routledge and Kegan Paul, 1973), 31, 35, 36, 492. In order to circumvent the problem posed by the élitism or difficulty of Morris's literary works, it might be tempting to argue that they were in fact quite deliberately aimed at an educated audience in order to 'raise the consciousness' of that audience *vis-à-vis* socialist politics. Such a view would, however, be totally at odds with Morris's claims both for his own art, and for art works in general.
4. Egbert, 445.
5. On this issue Peter Faulkner, for example, merely comments vaguely: 'The question goes deep, and is related to the coexistence in Morris of a love of some aspects of history and an intense concern about the future of humanity.' See Peter Faulkner, *Against the Age* (London: Allen and Unwin, 1980), 129. A more typical reaction is that of Margaret Grennan who explains Morris's late literary works as a diversion, or 'escape' from politics, 'never intended to "delight the naïve minds of the Victorian working classes" . . . [but] intended, rather, to delight William Morris and those who could follow him in his knowledge of the romantic tradition.' See Margaret Grennan, *William Morris: Medievalist and revolutionary* (New York: King's Crown Press, 1954), 106. Other studies of Morris's literature have failed to address this issue altogether. Alice Chandler, for example, has discussed the politics of Morris's prose romances in terms of their content and so has largely ignored the difficulties which their form presents. Amanda Hodgson, on the other hand, by concentrating on the aesthetic or literary qualities of these works has tended to marginalise their political impact. In her eyes the overt propaganda of *The Dream of John Ball* and *News From Nowhere* debars them from being true romances; hence for her the problems raised by those politics are irrelevant. See Alice Chandler, *A Dream of Order: The medieval ideal in nineteenth-century literature* (London: Routledge and Kegan Paul, 1971) and Amanda Hodgson, *The Romances of William Morris* (Cambridge: Cambridge University Press, 1987). An exception to these tendencies, which I refer to later in this chapter, is John Goode. Contrasting Morris's prose romances with works by writers such as Gissing, Hardy and James, Goode argues that Morris's choice of the romance form, rather than the devices of realism used by some of his contemporaries, far from being 'a mere relief from or appendage to his directly active work as a Socialist in the eighties' was a reasoned and appropriate response to 'the realities of his own situation':

> Morris's Romances are attempts to give concrete expression to values which are best seen in possibilities offered by defeated social orders, but also to recreate those orders so that they speak to the dreams of the estranged man not merely as something gone but as something containing values that must be striven after, and can be attained only by the transformation of dream into vision.

See John Goode, 'William Morris and the Dream of Revolution' in John Lucas (ed.), *Literature and Politics in the Nineteenth Century* (London: Methuen, 1971), 221–78.

6. See E. P. Thompson, *William Morris: Romantic to revolutionary* (London: Lawrence Wishart, 1955); Paul Meier, *William Morris: The Marxist dreamer*, 2 vols. (Brighton: Harvester, 1978); and Raymond Williams, *Culture and Society* (Harmondsworth: Chatto and Windus, 1968). Williams's comments may stand for all three:

> For my own part, I would willingly lose *The Dream of John Ball* and the romantic socialist songs and even *News from Nowhere* – in all of which the weaknesses of Morris's general poetry are active and disabling – if to do so were the price of retaining and getting people to read such smaller things as *How we Live*, and *How we might Live*, *The Aims of Art*, *Useless Work versus Useless Toil*, and *A Factory as it Might Be*. (158)

7. Goode, 222.
8. In this respect it is worth noting that Egbert's definition of avant-gardism was purposely narrow – the tracing of radical political views held by artists and writers in Western Europe; how those radical views were represented in art and literature was not of interest to him.
9. Thompson, 773.
10. Morris, 'How we Live & How we might Live', *Collected Works*, XXIII, 3.
11. Morris, 'Art Under Plutocracy', *Collected Works*, XXIII, 189. It is interesting to note also that Morris chose the decline of the Roman Empire as a metaphor for revolutionary change. (See 'Art and Socialism', *Collected Works*, XXIII, 204.) During the 1880s, as Linda Dowling has argued, Roman historiography underwent some fundamental changes central to which was the idea, taken from the German scholar, Theodor Mommsen, that the history of Rome was in fact characterised by the continuity of its institutions rather than by a 'decline and fall'. See Linda Dowling, 'Roman decadence and Victorian historiography', *Victorian Studies*, 28 (1985), 579–607.
12. Morris, 'Paper read at the seventh annual meeting of the SPAB, 1 July 1884', *William Morris: Artist, Writer, Socialist*, ed. May Morris (Oxford: Basil Blackwell, 1936), I, 124.
13. Morris, 'How we Live & How we might Live', 25.
14. Morris, 'Address at the twelfth annual meeting, 3 July 1889', *William Morris: Artist, Writer, Socialist*, I, 152.
15. See Thompson, 277.
16. Morris, 'The English Pre-Raphaelite School', *William Morris: Artist, Writer, Socialist*, I, 297–8.
17. Morris, 'Papers on arts and crafts: Gothic architecture', *William Morris: Artist, Writer, Socialist*, I, 285.
18. See in particular Thompson and Meier, op. cit.
19. Morris, 'The English Pre-Raphaelite School', 297.
20. William Michael Rossetti, 'The Brotherhood in a nutshell', *The Germ*,

(1850). Quoted in Derek Stanford (ed.), *Pre-Raphaelite Writing* (London: Dent, 1973), 16.

21. F. G. Stephens, 'The purpose and tendency of early Italian art', *The Germ* (1850). Quoted in James Sambrook (ed.), *Pre-Raphaelitism* (London: University of Chicago Press, 1974), 57.

22. Ibid.

23. William Holman Hunt, *Pre-Raphaelitism and the Pre-Raphaelite Brotherhood* (London: Macmillan, 1905). Quoted in Sambrook, 337.

24. *The Times*, (7 May 1851). Quoted in Stanford, 331.

25. William Michael Rossetti, 'The Brotherhood in a nutshell'. Quoted in Stanford, 15.

26. Morris, 'The English Pre-Raphaelite School', 308.

27. Morris, 'The Lesser Arts', *Collected Works*, XXII, 16.

28. Ibid. 12.

29. See Margaret Grennan, *William Morris*, op. cit.

30. Morris, 'Art and its producers', *Collected Works*, XXII, 345–6.

31. See Charles Dellheim, *The Face of the Past: The preservation of the medieval inheritance in Victorian Britain* (Cambridge: Cambridge University Press, 1982).

32. Grennan, 62.

33. A similar kind of argument has been set out by John Goode (op. cit.). He suggests that Morris used the narrative structures of dream and vision in order to 'dramatize the tensions in the revolutionary mind' and so to overcome the 'theoretically insoluble' epistemological problem in Marxist accounts of art of the relationship between determining processes and individual consciousness. What Goode does not explain is *why* Morris's 'formal experiments' of the 1880s were based on reworkings of old devices except in the weak sense that these devices were a more useful means of dramatising these tensions than those of realism. Nor indeed can Goode account for the linguistic archaisms of Morris's style which he describes as 'opaque and frequently inept – a combination of pseudo-anachronism trying to escape from the realities of modern English.' (239)

34. Morris, 'Address at the twelfth annual meeting, 3 July 1889', 148.

35. Grennan, 94.

36. For an account of the 'more purely imaginative approach' of the last romances, see Hodgson, 157 ff.

37. Morris, 'The Lesser Arts', 26.

38. Unsigned review, *Nation*, 63 (1896), 88. Quoted in Faulkner (ed.), *William Morris: The critical heritage*, 388.

39. Oscar Wilde, 'The English Renaissance of Art' in Oscar Wilde, *Essays and Lectures* (1908; London: Methuen, 1913), 122. 'The English Renaissance of Art' was first delivered as a lecture in New York on 9 January 1882. A portion of it was reported in the *New York Times* the following day, and was subsequently reprinted from time to time in unauthorised editions.

CHAPTER 7

Oscar Wilde:
'Traditional iconoclast'

Although Wilde is widely recognised as one of the nineteenth century's most conspicuous iconoclasts, he is rarely acknowledged to be an avant-garde writer. The reasons are not hard to find. Wilde's radicalism simply elides the differences between the categories into which avant-garde activity is generally placed. It is difficult, for example, to find consistent evidence of radical political thinking in his work. Only *Vera, or the Nihilists*, his privately printed and unperformed play, has an overt political subject. Even then the 'seriousness' of those politics – a form of aristocratic socialism distilled from Wilde's interests in anarchism, socialism and democracy – is severely compromised by the play's melodramatic formal devices. As Katherine Worth has noted, the revolutionary rhetoric is too easily and too often sacrificed to the passion and sensationalism characteristic of the genre.[1] In addition, it is equally difficult to find evidence of formal innovation in Wilde's work; his writing is too derivative, too free in the formal conventions it borrows for such a judgement. Even *Salomé*, clearly Wilde's most innovative play, borrows heavily from other traditions and from other writers. Its subject matter owes much to Huysmans's *A Rebours* and Laforgue's *Moralités Légendaires*, Mallarmé's *Hérodiade*, Flaubert's *Hérodias* and Massenet's *Hérodiade*; and elements of its imagery to Maeterlincks's *La Princesse Maleine* and Moreau's painting, *The Apparition*.[2] In this respect it is not surprising that in recent years Wilde's radicalism has tended to engage the attention of critics interested in his sexual politics, for in this view it is Wilde's confrontation with Victorian sexual orthodoxies, rather than literary traditions which is of primary interest. Such an argument may make Wilde radical in his views on sex and gender, but it has little to say about his literary radicalism.[3] A final, but by no means unimportant, problem in locating Wilde within a tradition of avant-garde writing concerns 'the life'. An ardent self-publicist, who at times went out of his way to court popularity, Wilde, rather like Courbet, ill fits the traditional image of the embattled 'anti-bourgeois' artist: the ironic detachment of the dandy, defined by those very bourgeois codes he rejects, is a far cry both from Poggioli's notion of 'alienation' and Bürger's of 'social praxis'.

When it has been discussed, Wilde's literary radicalism has generally, if somewhat paradoxically, been located in what appear to be his most 'conventional' works – the society comedies. The radicalism of these plays has usually been seen in terms of strategies of appropriation and subversion. So Russell Jackson, for example, has described how Wilde uses conventional dramatic forms, such as those borrowed from melodrama and the French 'well-made play', but in contexts which subvert their traditional significance.[4] Thus the improbability of the plot resolution in the final act of *An Ideal Husband*, and the self-conscious contrivance with which it is achieved, can be seen as undermining the notion of social cohesion which such formal devices were traditionally held to confirm. This kind of argument may usefully alert us to the serious and subversive side to the society comedies, the politics of which, as Jackson has noted, have tended in the passing of time to become 'harmless'.[5] However, it will not by itself make a very strong case for Wilde being considered an avant-garde writer. A weak (but not insignificant) argument may be made concerning Wilde's avant-gardism within British dramatic tradition. Even then, however, such a view is only possible given the defining context of the extreme conservatism of the work of contemporaries such as Arthur Wing Pinero and Henry Arthur Jones.

As theatre historians have pointed out, nineteenth-century British dramatists wrote under an unusually restrictive set of constraints. As well as the formal censorship that operated through the Lord Chamberlain's licence, there was also a series of informal impositions. The involvement of the new breed of actor-managers in the production of the play (and in Wilde's case, probably the production of parts of the text itself) and the demands of a highly conservative West End audience, all placed severe limits on the extent of dramatic invention.[6] The failure of *Vera, or the Nihilists*, Wilde's first experiment in 'political' drama, and the failure too of *Salomé*, his most ambitious aesthetic or formal experiment, bear out this point. Both plays were cancelled during the first few weeks of rehearsal; indeed the latter was refused a licence by the Lord Chamberlain's Office. On the publication of *Salomé* the following year, critical reaction was hardly more favourable; most reviewers either pointedly ignored the play or treated it with open contempt. Wilde's comment at the time on the 'official tyranny that exists in England in reference to the drama' may thus be taken seriously;[7] it is significant that *Salomé* received its first (private) staging in France in the same year, 1896, that Wilde was in prison in England. The rejection of *Salomé* in Britain, and its enthusiastic reception in France and Germany (particularly by Strauss) is thus further testimony to the uniqueness of the intellectual conditions for avant-garde activity in Britain; what was an 'appropriate' form of opposition in France, was simply unacceptable in Britain. In view of these conditions, then, we should not expect to find the same degree (or kind) of radicalism in drama as in other literary forms in Britain; but if this is the case, neither should we look to Wilde's plays for the best examples of his literary radicalism. (As I have suggested, however, this is not to deny that there are radical and original elements, both 'political' and 'aesthetic', in Wilde's plays.)[8]

To make a strong argument concerning Wilde's status as an avant-garde writer involves considering other aspects of his *oeuvre*; but here there seems to be another intractable problem. Wilde's work is well-known for its plagiarisms, *Intentions* and *The Picture of Dorian Gray* providing the most notorious examples. Ideas of plagiarism and avant-garde originality consort oddly. Moreover, the derivative qualities of these and other works clearly cannot be explained in terms of 'special circumstances' such as those which affected the production of theatrical texts in Britain. To explain the strategies which informed these works – to see in what ways they might be considered innovative or radical – we must look elsewhere. The answer is in fact provided by the general intellectual constraints which I have described in earlier chapters. The forms of Wilde's radicalism – the ways in which, as I shall indicate, he attempted to undermine the authority of traditions by using his sources to create 'new' works – can be traced to a general attitude towards the past which informed the culture in which he was working; and, more precisely, to his view of the vexed relationship in Britain between the innovative writer and tradition. This attitude was brought about by the general conservatism which I have suggested characterised late nineteenth-century Britain. Wilde, like his contemporaries, had to find means of expressing his opposition to social and literary norms in ways other than those practised by the French avant-garde artists and writers he clearly admired, but whose example was inappropriate to a British context.

Wilde's solution to the problem of innovation in a culture where the authority of tradition was dominant was characteristically flamboyant: 'it is only the unimaginative who ever invent', he argued, 'the true artist is known by the use he makes of what he annexes, and he annexes everything'.[9] The paradox is of course typical; and the sentiment, too, is not unique. Wilde is simply laying bare the general principle of the appropriation and reinterpretation of traditions which had guided the more covert 'rehabilitations' of Pater and Morris; his singularity lies in the particularly blatant use he made of the strategy. As I have indicated, Pater and Morris invoked a tradition in order to disguise or deny the innovative aspects of their thinking; in this sense traditions lent authority to Pater's and Morris's idiosyncratic (and subversive) views about the nature and function of art and literature by appearing to invoke historical precedents for those views. Wilde, on the other hand, uses exactly the same general strategy, but he does so in order to *exhibit* his originality: what Pater and Morris had disguised, he holds up for general inspection. Wilde claimed that in the hands of the 'true' artist all traditions were transformed into something new, and that they had authority only in so far as they 'bore the signature' of the artist who interpreted them. In Wilde's view, then, no less than Pater's, it was the activities of the contemporary artist which authorised traditions, rather than the opposite – those traditions authorising contemporary activities. Far from possessing a normative function, for Wilde, traditions were merely the 'suggestion' for an entirely new creation.

Wilde's view of the vexed relationship between the innovative artist and tradition is elaborated most fully in the discussion of creativity in 'The Critic as Artist'. However, a comment in the slightly earlier essay, 'The Soul of Man Under Socialism', is useful in that it allows us to see what for him was the central issue in this relationship. In the context of a general discussion of the nature and exercise of authority, Wilde draws attention to the singularity of the role played by traditions in the field of art and literature:

> The fact is, the public make use of the classics of a country as a means of checking the progress of Art. They degrade the classics into authorities. They use them as bludgeons for preventing the free expression of Beauty in new forms. They are always asking a writer why he does not write like somebody else, or a painter why he does not paint like somebody else, quite oblivious of the fact that if either of them did anything of the kind he would cease to be an artist. . . . The true artist is a man who believes absolutely in himself, because he is absolutely himself.[10]

The situation which Wilde describes was exactly that so successfully exploited by Pater; Pater's use of Plato to mark out a 'constant tradition' of Aestheticism played upon precisely that general, uncritical acceptance of 'classical authority' which Wilde openly deplores. In contrast to Pater's careful sleight-of-hand, then, Wilde adopts a more provocative position. As I have noted, by revealing Pater's apparent respect for tradition to be the manipulative strategy it really was, Wilde proposes that authority be removed from traditions altogether and placed instead in the hands of the contemporary artist. In Wilde's view, traditions were nothing more than the artist's raw 'materials'; and it was the artist's unique handling of them – the extent to which he transformed them through the exercise of his personality, and therefore his style – which was of primary interest. Indeed Wilde (once more like Pater) enlists no lesser figures than Homer and Shakespeare to make his point: 'No doubt Homer had old ballads and stories to deal with, as Shakespeare had chronicles and plays and novels from which to work, but they were merely his rough material. He took them, and shaped them . . . [and] they become his.'[11] Traditions in themselves, then, had no inherent value; rather it was the 'treatment' of them which assigned significance to them.

All these points are discussed in 'The Critic as Artist' where Wilde famously broadens the notion of artistic creation to include the practice of criticism itself. For Wilde, criticism was simply art at its most innovative. 'It is to criticism that the future belongs', he argued, 'if creation is to last at all, it can only do so on the condition of becoming far more critical than it is at present'.[12] Such an elevated claim for the innovative power of criticism should not, however, come as any surprise. Like most of Wilde paradoxes, the suggestion that criticism was 'more creative than creation' had a serious, and even a prosaic side. If artistic innovation was to be defined in Britain in terms of the transformative use of traditions then clearly the critic, as a licensed, legitimate, or 'professional' interpreter of traditions was, as Wilde suggested, best placed to invent 'fresh forms'.[13] Having discovered for himself that literary criticism was a more suitable vehicle for the expression of radical views than other literary forms (especially, as I have suggested, that of drama), it is to be expected that Wilde should set out a theoretical justification for the importance of the critic's – that is, Wilde's own – role in contemporary society.

One of the central themes in the dialogue between Ernest and Gilbert is the idea of 'borrowing', or – to use the pejorative term – plagiarism. Early in the essay Wilde argues that such an allegation when directed at the artist (or critic), is entirely misplaced. Indeed such views are testimony only to the 'inartistic temperaments' of those who hold them. The point is made in the context of Gilbert's discussion of the state of criticism in ancient Greece.

> The accusations of plagiarism were endless, and such accusations proceeded either from the thin colourless lips of impotence, or from the grotesque mouths of those who, possessing nothing of their own, fancy they can gain a reputation for wealth by crying out that they have been robbed.[14]

The comment was particularly apt coming from a writer with a reputation as 'a fearless literary thief'. A further comment which Robert Ross alleges Wilde made to him clinches this point about artistic 'annexing' (or 'borrowing' or 'plagiarism') very neatly: 'when I see a monstrous tulip with *four* petals in someone else's garden, I am impelled to grow a monstrous tulip with *five* wonderful petals, but that is no reason why someone should grow a tulip with only *three* petals.'[15] Wilde's point is that the artist who 'borrows' does so only in order to improve on his source, to create something new from it. It is the uniqueness of the new creation which liberates the writer from what Pater had described in *Marius* as 'the burden of precedent', and which therefore nullifies any accusation of plagiarism. Another writer's ideas become the borrower's own only to the extent that he succeeds in transforming them into something new. Wilde made the point in more general terms when he claimed that 'the one duty we owe to history is to re-write it. That is not the least of the tasks in store for the critical spirit.'[16] Quite appropriately, the comment had had an earlier existence in his essay, 'The Rise of Historical Criticism' where its subversive nature was made quite explicit: 'Historical criticism', Wilde argues, is 'part of that complex working towards freedom which may be described as the revolt against authority.'[17]

Wilde's creative 'annexing', to use his own phrase, operates at three levels in his work: in his appropriation and transformation of the ideas and theories of his predecessors, most famously those of Pater and Arnold; in his unconventional use of various formal conventions and genres; and in his subversion of the traditional vocabulary and concepts used to define such subjects as art and morality. All these practices have of course on their own received attention from a number of critics – but they have yet to be explained as instances of a single, coherent strategy of opposition to the past, one which links Wilde's work to other avant-garde writers in Britain. When Wilde's originality or radicalism is assessed in his own terms – in terms, that is, of the extent to which he was able to transform those traditions which he 'annexed' – the problem of how to incorporate his work within a history of avant-gardism is easily resolved.

The first kind of annexation, as I have suggested, is best exemplified by Wilde's use of Pater and Arnold in *Intentions*; indeed the presence of these two figures in Wilde's text has probably received more attention than any of his other borrowings.[18] It was certainly widely commented upon at the time. The reviewer for the *Pall Mall Gazette*, for example, described Wilde as possessing 'every qualification for becoming a popular Pater', later adding the astute witticism that if Wilde 'would condescend to suppress some over-complacent allusions to the artistic value of "sin" – a favourite word of his – he might fairly be described as a Pater-familias.'[19] The same point was picked up by the reviewer in the *Athenaeum*, but this time apropos of Wilde's use of Arnold: 'When [Wilde] speaks of Matthew Arnold's definition of "literature" as a criticism of life he is worse than reckless[;] . . . he shows, perhaps, that strict accuracy is beneath him.'[20] Richard Le Gallienne, in his review for the *Academy*, had referred in more polite terms to Wilde as 'a damascener of thought, [rather] than a forger of it'.[21] All, then, noticed the pervasiveness of Wilde's borrowings; but all noticed too their unusual nature: Wilde had not simply repeated ideas and theories of Arnold and Pater; he had subtly but significantly transformed them.

To take Pater first. In Wilde's hands, Pater's fastidious impressionist aesthetic had become a justification for sin: crime itself, Wilde seemed to suggest in 'Pen, Pencil and Poison', was capable of being aestheticised:

> His [Wainewright's] crimes seem to have had an important effect upon his art. They gave a strong personality to his style, a quality that his early work certainly lacked . . . . There is no essential incongruity between crime and culture. We cannot re-write the whole of history for the purpose of gratifying our moral sense of what should be.[22]

One of the striking features of the essay is the absence of any real attempt to disguise either the references to Pater himself (in the portrait of Wainewright) or the borrowings from his work. At one point, for example, Wainewright is described as attempting 'to revive style as a conscious tradition'; and a less flattering, but equally knowing allusion was contained in the essay's subtitle, 'A Study in Green'. Green was a colour popularly associated with the members of the Aesthetic Movement; Wilde himself was to wear a green carnation (a 'symbol' of homosexuality) at the first night of *Lady Windermere's Fan*. Similarly, whole phrases and concepts are taken from *The Renaissance* with an insouciant self-consciousness uncharacteristic of the straightforward plagiarist: 'an art critic', Wilde comments at one point, is 'concerned . . . primarily with the complex impressions produced by a work of art, and certainly the first step in aesthetic criticism is to realise one's own impressions. . . . Art's first appeal is . . . purely to the artistic temperament.'[23] The significance of Pater's work in Wilde's argument depends upon its transparency, upon, that is, an *immediate* recognition of where the allusions come from, for Wilde's point here, and with other of his borrowings, is to invite the reader to see how he has transformed familiar theories and ideas by placing them in different contexts. Through exercising the 'spirit of choice' or 'subtle tact of omission', practices which Wilde had described as characteristic of the critical or creative faculty, he transforms Pater's theory of aesthetic perception into something altogether more sinister and subversive. Wilde thus exhibits his innovative qualities by explicitly inviting a comparison with his predecessor; 'the old' – that is, Pater's theory of aesthetic perception – functions to reveal the 'newness' of the new – Wilde's aestheticising of sin. In this way Wilde reverses the conventional relationship between the contemporary writer and tradition; far from Pater authorising Wilde, it is Wilde who gives significance to Pater by setting his theories in a new and radical light.

In Wilde's use of Arnold in 'The Critic as Artist' a similar process is at work. Here the central paradox of the dialogue is that 'the highest aim of criticism . . . is more creative than creation, and [that] the primary aim of the critic is to see the object as in itself it really is not'; and it is developed in the context of Arnold's famous argument about the role of the critic set out in 'The Function of Criticism at the Present Time'. The acknowledgement of Arnold's 'influence', like that of Pater in 'Pen, Pencil and Poison', is made explicitly quite early in the dialogue, but in such a way as to signal very precisely the way in which Wilde was to use Arnold: 'Arnold's definition of literature as a criticism of life was not very felicitous in form', Wilde argues, 'but it showed how keenly he recognised the importance of the critical element in all creative work'.[24] This point is subsequently applied in such an original way that Arnold's comment about the relationship between literature and life is totally controverted. This is made explicit in a famous passage in the dialogue:

> *Gilbert*: Yes: it has been said by one whose gracious memory we all revere . . . that the proper aim of Criticism is to see the object as in itself it really is. But this is a very serious error, and takes no cognisance of Criticism's most perfect form, which is in its essence purely subjective, and seeks to reveal its own secret and not the secret of another. . . .
> *Ernest*: The highest Criticism, then, is more creative than creation, and the primary aim of the critic is to see the object as in itself is really is not . . . ?
> *Gilbert*: Yes, that is my theory.[25]

For Wilde, Arnold's theories are 'useful' only to the extent that he can transform them; the significance – or authority – of Arnold's injunction to the critic, 'to see the object as in itself it really is,' lies in the way in which it becomes 'a suggestion for a new work', the corollary, that is, of Wilde's proposal that the aim of the critic is 'to see the object as in itself is really is not'. Arnold's theories, then, like those of Pater, are in the first place a vehicle for the exhibition of Wilde's originality. Indeed as the dialogue progresses the Arnoldian echoes become increasingly dense and Wilde's reworking of the essay of his predecessor more knowing: 'the critic may, indeed, desire to exercise influence', Wilde argues at one point, alluding to the argument of 'The Function of Criticism at the Present Time', 'but, if so, he will concern himself not with the individual, but with the age, which he will seek to awake into consciousness, and to make responsive, creating in it new desires and appetites, and lending it his larger vision and his nobler moods.' In his deliberate and undisguised manipulation of Arnold's arguments Wilde is putting into practice his own proposal that, for the critic or artist, the work of one's predecessors, like those chronicles and novels 'used' by Shakespeare, are nothing more than 'materials'. And as materials, they are open to be 'shaped' in whatever way the critic or artist sees fit.

What is striking, then, in Wilde's borrowings from Pater and Arnold is his willingness to acknowledge, indeed to exhibit, his sources; and it is this self-consciousness which nullifies any simple accusations of plagiarism and self-advertisement. Although we may not necessarily agree that Wilde fully succeeds in *Intentions* in creating, to use his term, a 'five-petalled' theory of art from the 'four-petalled' ones of Pater and Arnold, it should nevertheless be recognised that this was Wilde's ambition in his conspicuous 'use' of the ideas of his predecessors.

As well as illustrating his transformative use of the ideas and theories of other writers, *Intentions* also provides an example of the second kind of annexing in Wilde's work, his unconventional use of certain formal conventions. In presenting his theories of life and art in 'The Critic as Artist' and 'The Decay of Lying' Wilde borrows one of the oldest and indeed most authoritative forms of critical debate – that of the philosophical dialogue. His reasons for so doing are made clear in the first essay:

> *Gilbert*: . . . By its [the Dialogues's] means he [the critic] can both reveal and conceal himself, and give form to every fancy, and reality to every mood. By its means he can exhibit the object from every point of view, and show it to us in the round, as a sculptor shows us things, gaining in this manner all the richness and reality of effect that comes from those side issues that are suddenly suggested by the central idea in its progress, and really illumine the idea more completely, or from those felicitous after-thoughts that give a fuller completeness to the central scheme, and yet convert something of the delicate charm of chance.

Ernest: By its means, too, he can invent an imaginary antagonist, and convert him when he chooses by some absurdly sophistical argument.[26]

The above, as Edward Watson has suggested, serves as a fairly accurate description of the function of the dialogue form in Wilde's own essay.[27] 'The form of the Dialogue', Watson argues, 'enables Wilde to engage in a variety of strategic ambiguities where the fictive elements fade into truth and truths into fictions, and implicit moral standards are maintained without either speaker having to prove his statements.'[28] 'It is consistent that the "creative critic"', Watson continues, 'utilizes a form which had been historically sanctioned and shares its antiquity with such other traditional forms as the drama and the epos.' Watson then briefly compares Wilde's use of the dialogue form with the Platonic prototype, concluding that in the hands of Wilde it:

> is used as a creative medium more so than as an instructional one: the *eiron* is no longer seen as an opponent, *per se*, but as representing the other half of consciousness when the matter of TRUTH remained a slippery, shadowy thing. Hence the Dialogue afforded Wilde the opportunity to both 'yea' say and 'nay' say within a provocative, creative context.[29]

The significant point about Wilde's borrowing of this convention lies, then, like his borrowings from Pater and Arnold, in the way in which he transforms it to suit his own purposes; indeed Wilde explicitly acknowledges the possibility of blatant authorial manipulation in his comment 'by some absurdly sophistical argument'. In exploiting the dramatic possibilities of the dialogue, Wilde thus uses the form to demonstrate the unfixed, relative nature of truth. (It might be noted, for example, that one of the features of 'The Critic as Artist' is the difficulty we have in identifying either speaker with a consistent point of view.)

Success in transforming sources and conventions is more assured in Wilde's fiction, particularly in his novel, *The Picture of Dorian Gray*. Here there is a wide agreement that 'despite its extraordinary reliance on previous fiction, *Dorian Gray* remains a brilliantly original novel'.[30] In it Wilde seems to have taken his own proposition that the 'true' artist 'annexes everything' fairly literally; research has revealed parallels with, and allusions to, figures as diverse as Poe, Huysmans, George Sala, Goethe, Gibbon, Balzac,

Disraeli, Walpole, Bulwer-Lytton, Robert Louis Stevenson, William Sharp, Nietszche, Ovid, Pater, Suetonius, Dante Gabriel Rossetti, Tennyson, Maturin, Hawthorne and Zola.[31] Wilde's plundering of various genres and sub-genres has also been noted; some of the conventions of the Gothic novel, the 'decadent novel', Restoration Comedy, *Bildüngsroman*, spiritual biography and 'magic picture' novel all seem to have found their way into *Dorian Gray*.[32] Moreover, most of the critics who have patiently mined these sources have been united in agreeing with Kerry Powell that the point of interest in Wilde's many 'borrowings' is the 'complex and transformative use [he] makes of the literary past'; so, as Powell demonstrates apropos of Wilde's use of 'magic picture' novels, it is the ways in which Wilde extends, transforms and at times subverts the conventions he borrows which is of most significance: 'the novel's distinctiveness arises . . . from surpassing the hypnotic genre which partly inspired it', Powell argues, 'just as the achievement of *Earnest* is best measured by the extent to which it transcends Victorian farce rather than imitates it'.[33] It is sufficient to note here that in *Dorian Gray*, Wilde's tactics, far from being 'extraordinary' (as Powell suggests) were simply a more accomplished and flamboyant example of a strategy which he employed throughout his work. Pater saw exactly the motive behind the writing of *Dorian Gray* in his review of the novel in 1891: 'side by side with Mr. Wilde's *Intentions* . . . comes a novel, certainly original, and affording the reader a fair opportunity of comparing his practice as a creative artist with many a precept he has enounced as critic concerning it.'[34] The enduring interest which the novel holds today lies in the complexity of its parody and plagiarism. A thief of so many literary genres, *Dorian Gray*, as Ian Fletcher and John Stokes have noted, fits none of them. Wilde's programme for the innovative artist, to create something new from the materials or traditions available, seems then to have been perfectly realised: in the terms which he set himself, that is, the novel is an original.

The final area of Wilde's annexing, his use and subversion of the traditional vocabulary and concepts used to define the nature and function of art, occurs throughout his work. However, one of the best, because most explicit, examples of this strategy is to be found in 'The Soul of Man Under Socialism'. Following his revaluation of plagiarism, Wilde engages with the critical terminology which he claims is commonly levelled at novel or innovative work: 'grossly immoral', 'grossly unintelligible', 'morbid', 'unhealthy', and 'exotic'.[35] All these terms, as I have indicated in earlier chapters, were employed in the debates about obscurity in the 1870s and 1880s; and all, especially that of 'unintelligible', had been resisted by figures such as Pater, Rossetti and Swinburne. Wilde, then, in attempting to revalue them, was merely continuing a tradition of avant-garde critique, although his particular contribution to this tradition was, like his adoption of other avant-garde strategies, characteristically extreme.

Pater's 'rehabilitation' of Wordsworth, as I have suggested, attempted covertly to reverse the usual oppositions which character-ised literariness; he had, for example, linked the concept of 'sincerity' with those of 'originality' and 'individuality'. In so doing he had appeared to suggest that it was not so much that the concepts commonly employed to characterise art were inappropriate ones; rather it was that they had been radically misunderstood. Wilde takes a similar line of argument, although again he is more explicit about the nature and extent of this misunderstanding. One example, his revaluation of the term 'unhealthy', will indicate his general strategy:

> What does it mean? What is a healthy or an unhealthy work of art? All terms that one applies to a work of art, provided that one applies them rationally, have reference to either its style or its subject, or to both together. . . . [A] healthy work of art is one whose style recognises the beauty of the material it employs, . . . [and] whose subject is conditioned by the temperament of the artist, and comes directly out of it. . . . An unhealthy work of art is a work whose style is obvious, old-fashioned and common, and whose subject is deliberately chosen, not because the artist has any pleasure in it, but because he thinks that the public will pay him for it. In fact, the popular novel that the public call an healthy novel is always a thoroughly unhealthy production; and what the public call an unhealthy novel is always a beautiful and healthy work of art.[36]

Wilde's strategy, like Pater's, is to redefine the 'literary' by using conventional or traditional concepts in unconventional ways.[37] The difference is that what in Pater was executed by a careful understatement is actually flaunted by Wilde through wit and paradox. The basic strategy, though, of reinterpreting traditions in terms of contemporary concerns, remains a constant one, both in Wilde's work and in that of the other members of the late nineteenth-century British literary avant-garde.

To argue that a figure as notorious for his plagiarism as Wilde, should in fact be considered an avant-garde writer may seem perverse. However, the ways in which Wilde systematically set out to remove authority from tradition by blatantly and self-consciously re-writing the work of his predecessors, give him as great a claim to that title as any of the other writers discussed here. Although there may be disagreement over the 'success' of Wilde's transformative use of his sources – disagreement, that is, as to the extent to which, in his terms, his individual works are 'original' – it should nevertheless be recognised that in reversing the usual relationship between a writer and tradition, Wilde had sanctioned literary and artistic innovation. Freed from the normative constraints of 'the burden of precedent', and free to interpret the past as he liked, the artist was, in Wilde's terms, truly his own authority – someone 'who believes absolutely in himself, because he is absolutely himself'.

Notes

1. See Katherine Worth's discussion of the play in *Oscar Wilde* (London: Macmillan, 1983). Worth also notes that where Wilde does attempt to overcome the limitations of this form by the introduction of Prince Paul Maraloffski, one of his earliest dandies, the problems are merely compounded. Next to Maraloffski's epigrammatic wit Vera's rhetoric sounds inflated, and the revolutionary enthusiasm of her compatriots merely naïve. The fact that such a 'wretched' play, as Richard Ellmann has called it, failed to find a British stage is testimony less to the radicalism of its content and more to the conservatism of the theatrical establishment.
2. To indicate *Salomé*'s many debts to other writers and traditions is not to deny its originality. In his use of triple form, in his employment of an elaborate symbolic structure – particularly the colour symbolism which was carried through to the highly stylised set designs and costumes in an attempt to create a 'total' theatre, and in his attempt to stylise the rhythm of speech, Wilde has been credited with having created from his sources 'a truly modern symbolist drama'. See Peter Raby, *Oscar Wilde* (Cambridge: Cambridge University Press, 1988); and Katherine Worth, op. cit.
3. See for example, Jonathan Dollimore, 'Different desires: subjectivity and transgression in Wilde and Gide', *Textual Practice*, 1 (1987), 48–67; Richard Dellamora, *Masculine Desire* (Chapel Hill and London: University of North Carolina Press, 1990); and Ed Cohen, 'Writing gone Wilde: homoerotic desire in the closet of representation', *PMLA*, 102 (1987), 801–13. It is also worth drawing attention to Regenia

Gagnier's recent and rather different account of Wilde's radicalism. Locating Wilde's work within the context of what she characterises as the emergence of a consumerist culture, Gagnier argues that its radicalism can be seen in the ways in which it subverts the materialist ideologies of that new culture. Her argument is strongest in the discussion of *De Profundis*; but for an account of Wilde's avant-gardism, that strength is also a weakness. Clearly an explanation, however convincing, of the radicalism of only one of Wilde's works – and one which itself is the most anomalous in his *oeuvre* – will not make a strong enough case for locating him within a history of avant-gardism. On the contrary: it tends rather to confirm the views of those historians who have seen Wilde as a marginal figure. See Regenia Gagnier, 'De Profundis as Epistola: *In Carcere et Vinculis*: a materialist reading of Oscar Wilde's autobiography', *Criticism*, 26 (1984), 335–54; and *Idylls of the Market Place: Oscar Wilde and the Victorian public* (Aldershot: Scolar, 1987).

4. See the Introduction to Russell Jackson (ed.), *Oscar Wilde: The Importance of Being Earnest* (London: Ernest Benn, 1980).

5. Russell Jackson, 'A classic without danger: The National Theatre's *Importance of Being Earnest*', *Critical Quarterly*, 25 (1983), 73–80.

6. See, for example, Russell Jackson, *Victorian Theatre* (London: A. and C. Black, 1989).

7. The comment was made in a letter to William Archer thanking him for his vigorous protest against the ban on *Salomé* in the *Pall Mall Gazette* in July 1892. It is quoted in Karl Beckson, *Oscar Wilde: The critical heritage* (London: Routledge and Kegan Paul, 1970), 17.

8. The ways in which Wilde's manipulation of formal conventions marks off the society comedies from the work of more conservative contemporaries, dramatists such as Arthur Wing Pinero and Henry Arthur Jones has been discussed, as I have indicated, in the Introductions to Russell Jackson's and Ian Small's editions of the society comedies (London: Ernest Benn, 1980–3). But the most comprehensive account of Wilde's dramatic radicalism (both aesthetic and political) is to be found in Katherine Worth's *Oscar Wilde* (op. cit.). Worth notes in particular Wilde's attempt, especially in *Salomé*, to create a 'total theatre', his willingness to engage with contemporary social and political issues (most significantly in the early plays) and his interest in (and debts to) some of the themes and formal devices employed in the radical drama of Ibsen. These issues have been taken up by other critics, notably by Kerry Powell in 'Wilde and Ibsen', *English Literature in Transition*, 28 (1985), 224–42; and, more recently, by Peter Raby (op. cit.).

9. The comment appeared in a review by Wilde. It is quoted in Richard Ellmann, *Oscar Wilde* (London: Penguin, 1988), 358.

10. Oscar Wilde, 'The soul of man under socialism', *The Works of Oscar Wilde*, ed. G. F. Maine (London: Collins, 1949), 1031.

11. Wilde, 'The critic as artist', *Works*, 959–60.

12. Ibid. 993.

13. Ibid. 960.

14. Ibid. 958.

15. The comment and Wilde's alleged reply to it are recorded in Robert Ross's preface to his edition of *Salomé* in the *Complete Works* (London: Methuen and Co., 1912). They are quoted in Ellmann, 320.
16. 'The critic as artist', 962.
17. Wilde, 'The Rise of Historical Criticism', *Works*, 1044.
18. See, for example, Ernst Bendz, *The Influence of Pater and Matthew Arnold in the Prose Writings of Oscar Wilde* (London: H. Grevel and Co., 1914); Leonard Brown, 'Arnold's Succession', *Sewanee Review*, 42 (1934), 158–79; John Pick, 'Divergent disciples of Walter Pater', *Thought*, 23 (1948), 114–28; and Wendell Harris, 'Arnold, Pater, Wilde, and the Object as in Themselves They See It', *Studies in English Literature*, 11 (1971), 733–47.
19. Unsigned review, *Pall Mall Gazette* (12 May 1891). See Beckson, 91.
20. Unsigned review, *Athenaeum* (6 June 1891). See Beckson, 93.
21. Richard Le Gallienne, *Academy* (4 July 1891). See Beckson, 99.
22. Wilde, 'Pen, pencil and poison', *Works*, 946–7.
23. Ibid. 936.
24. Wilde, 'The critic as artist', *Works*, 959.
25. Ibid. 967 and 969.
26. Ibid. 985.
27. See Edward A. Watson, 'Wilde's iconoclastic classicism: "The Critic as Artist"', *English Literature in Transition*, 27 (1984), 225–35.
28. Ibid. 226.
29. Ibid. 226–7.
30. Kerry Powell, 'Tom, Dick, and Dorian Gray: magic-picture mania in late Victorian fiction', *Philological Quarterly*, 62 (1983), 148.
31. See, for example, Walther Fischer, 'The "Poisonous Book" in Oscar Wilde's *Dorian Gray*', *Englische Studien*, 51 (1917), 37–47; Lucius H. Cook, 'French sources of Wilde's *The Picture of Dorian Gray*', *Romantic Review*, 19 (1928), 25–34; R. D. Brown, 'Suetonius, Symonds and Gibbon in *The Picture of Dorian Gray*', *Modern Language Notes*, 71 (1956), 264; Oscar Maurer, 'A philistine source for *Dorian Gray*', *Philological Quarterly*, 26 (1947), 84–6; Houston A. Baker, 'A tragedy of the artist: *The Picture of Dorian Gray*', *Nineteenth Century Fiction*, 24 (1969), 349–55; Ted Spivey, 'Damnation and salvation in *The Picture of Dorian Gray*', *Boston University Studies in English*, 4 (1960), 162–70; Gerald Monsman, 'Pater's Aesthetic Hero', *University of Toronto Quarterly*, 40 (1971), 136–51; Isobel Murray, 'The strange case of Dr Jekyll and Oscar Wilde', *Durham University Journal*, 79 (1987a), 311–19, and '*Children of Tomorrow*: a Sharp inspiration for *Dorian Gray*', *Durham University Journal*, 80 (1987b), 69–76.
32. See, for example, Ian Fletcher and John Stokes, 'Oscar Wilde', in Richard Finneran (ed.), *Anglo-Irish Literature: A review of research* (New York: Modern Language Association of America, 1976), 108–12; Kerry Powell 'Magic Picture Mania' (op. cit.), and 'Hawthorne, Arlo Bates and *The Picture of Dorian Gray*', *Papers in Language and Literature*, 16 (1980), 403–16; and Nathan Corvo, 'Wilde's closet self: a solo at one remove', *Victorian Newsletter*, 67 (1985), 17–19.

33. Kerry Powell, 'The mesmerizing of Dorian Gray', *Victorian Newsletter*, 65 (1984), 20.
34. Walter Pater, 'A novel by Mr. Oscar Wilde', *Bookman* (November, 1981). Quoted in Beckson, 83.
35. Wilde, 'The soul of man under socialism', *Works*, 1031–3.
36. Ibid. 1032–3.
37. This strategy of using but subverting traditional concepts also underlies Wilde's use of paradox in general, and, in particular, his use of aphorisms in 'Phrases and Philosophies for the Use of the Young'. See Sandra Siegal, 'Wilde's use and abuse of aphorism', *Victorian Studies Association of Western Canada Newsletter*, 12 (1986), 16–26.

Bibliography

Abrams, Philip, *The Origins of British Sociology* (London: University of Chicago Press, 1968).

Adelman, Paul, 'Frederick Harrison and the "positivist" attack on orthodox political economy', *History of Political Economy*, 3 (1971), 170–89.

Adorno, Theodor, *Philosophy of Modern Music* (London: Sheed and Ward, 1973).

Allen, Grant, 'The decay of criticism', *Fortnightly Review*, 37 (1882), 339–51.

Allott, Miriam (ed.), *Matthew Arnold: Selected poems and prose* (London: J. M. Dent, 1978).

Althusser, Louis, *For Marx* (London: Penguin, 1969).

Anderson, Perry, *Considerations on Western Marxism* (London: New Left Books, 1978).

Appleman, Philip, 'Darwin and Pater's Critical Dilemma', *Darwin: A Norton critical edition*, ed. Philip Appleman (New York: Norton, 1970).

Arnold, Matthew, *Poems of Wordsworth* (London: Macmillan, 1879a).

Arnold, Matthew, 'Wordsworth', *Macmillan's Magazine*, 40 (1879b), 103–204.

Arnold, Matthew, *Culture and Anarchy*, ed. J. Dover Wilson (Cambridge: Cambridge University Press, 1984).

Aron, Raymond, *Main Currents in Sociological Thought* (London: Penguin, 1965).

Austin, Alfred, 'The poetry of the period', *Temple Bar*, 26 (1869), 316–33.

Baker, Houston A., 'A tragedy of the artist: *The Picture of Dorian Gray*', *Nineteenth Century Fiction*, 24 (1969), 349–55.

Bann, Stephen, *The Clothing of Clio* (Cambridge: Cambridge University Press, 1984).

Beckson, Karl, *Oscar Wilde: The critical heritage* (London: Routledge and Kegan Paul, 1970).

Ben-Israel, Hedva, *Historians on the French Revolution* (Cambridge: Cambridge University Press, 1968).

Bendz, Ernest, *The Influence of Pater and Matthew Arnold in the Prose Writings of Oscar Wilde* (London: H. Grevel and Co., 1914).

Birken, Lawrence, 'From macroeconomic to microeconomics: the marginalist revolution in sociocultural perspective', *History of Political Economy*, 20 (1988), 251–64.

Black, R. D. Collison, 'W. S. Jevons and the foundation of modern economics', *History of Political Economy*, 4 (1972), 365–78.

Black, R. D. Collison, A. W. Coats, Crawfurd D. W. Goodwin (eds.), *The Marginalist Revolution in Economics: Interpretation and evaluation* (Durham, N. Carolina: Duke University Press, 1973).

Blackhouse, Roger, *A History of Modern Economic Analysis* (Oxford: Basil Blackwell, 1985).

Blatt, Sidney J. (in collaboration with Ethel S. Blatt), *Continuity and Change in Art: The development of modes of representation* (Hillsdale, N.J.: Erlbaum, 1984).

Blaug, Mark, *Economic Theory in Retrospect* (Cambridge: Cambridge University Press, 1978).

Bloch, Ernst, Georg Lukács, Bertolt Brecht, Walter Benjamin and Theodor Adorno, *Aesthetics and Politics*, ed. and trans., Ronald Taylor (London: Verso, 1977).

Boch, Kenneth, *The Acceptance of Histories: Towards a perspective for social science*, *University of California Publications in Sociology and Social Institutions* (Berkeley and Los Angeles: University of California Press, 1956).

Boime, Alfred, *The Academy and French Painting in the Nineteenth Century* (London: Phaidon Press, 1971).

Breisach, Ernst, *Historiography: Ancient, medieval and modern* (London: University of Chicago Press, 1983).

Brown, Leonard, 'Arnold's Succession', *Sewanee Review*, 42 (1934), 158–79.

Brown, R. D., 'Suetonius, Symonds and Gibbon in *The Picture of Dorian Gray*', *Modern Language Notes*, 71 (1956), 264.

Browning Society Papers, 1–3 (1881–90).

Buchanan, Robert, The Athenaeum (20 March 1869), 399.

Buchanan, Robert, 'The Fleshly School of Poetry: Mr D. G. Rossetti', *Contemporary Review*, 18 (1871), 334–50.

Buckle, Henry Thomas, *History of Civilization in England*, 2 vols. (London: J. W. Parker, 1857–61).

Bürger, Peter, 'The significance of the avant-garde for contemporary aesthetics: A reply to Jürgen Habermas', *New German Critique*, 22 (Winter, 1981), 19–22.

Bürger, Peter, *Theory of the Avant-Garde* (Manchester: Manchester University Press, 1984).

Burrow, J. W., *Evolution and Society: A study in Victorian social theory* (Cambridge: Cambridge University Press, 1966).

Burrow, J. W., *A Liberal Descent: Victorians and the English past* (Cambridge: Cambridge University Press, 1981).

Butterfield, Herbert, 'Some trends in scholarship 1868–1968 in the field of modern history', *Transactions of the Royal Historical Society*, 5th series, 19 (1969), 159–84.

Butterfield, Herbert, 'Delays and paradoxes in the development of historiography' in K. Bourne and D. C. Watt (eds.), *Studies in International History* (London: Longman 1987), 1–15.

Cachin, François, 'The neo-impressionist avant-garde' in Hess and Ashbery (eds.), *The Avant-Garde, Art News Annual*, 34 (1968), 55–64.

Calinescu, Matei, *Faces of Modernity: Avant-Garde, Decadence, Kitsch* (Bloomington, Indiana: Indiana University Press, 1977).

Carlyle, Thomas, *The French Revolution: A history*, 3 vols. (London: James Fraser, 1837).

Chandler, Alice, *A Dream of Order: The medieval ideal in nineteenth-century literature* (London: Routledge and Kegan Paul, 1971).

Clark, T. J., *The Absolute Bourgeois: Artists and politics in France 1848–1851* (London: Thames and Hudson, 1971).

Clark, T. J., *Image of the People: Gustave Courbet and the 1848 Revolution* (London: Thames and Hudson, 1973).

Clements, Patricia, *Baudelaire and the English Tradition* (Princeton, N.J.: Princeton University Press, 1985).

Clough, Arthur Hugh, *Poems and Prose Remains* (London: Macmillan, 1869).

Coats, A. W., 'Sociological aspects of British economic thought (CA 1880–1930)', *Journal of Political Economy*, 75 (1967), 706–29.

Cohen, Ed, 'Writing gone Wilde: homoerotic desire in the closet of representation', *PMLA*, 102 (1987), 801–13.

Collingwood, W. G., *The Life and Work of John Ruskin*, 2 vols. (London: Methuen, 1893).

Collini, Stefan, Donald Winch, J. W. Burrow (eds.), *That Nobel Science of Politics* (Cambridge: Cambridge University Press, 1983).

Colls, Richard and Philip Dodd (eds.), *Englishness: Politics and culture 1880–1920* (London: Croom Helm, 1986).

Cook, Lucius H., 'French sources of Wilde's *The Picture of Dorian Gray*', *Romantic Review*, 19 (1928), 25–34.

Cork, Richard, *Vorticism and Abstract Art in the First Machine Age*, 2 vols. (London: Gordon Fraser, 1976).

Corvo, Nathan, 'Wilde's closet self: A solo at one remove', *Victorian Newsletter*, 67 (1985), 17–19.

Courthope, William J., 'Conservatism in art', *National Review*, 1 (1883a), 72–84.

Courthope, William J., ' "Jocoseria" and the critics: A plea for the reader', *National Review*, 1 (1883b), 548–61.

Crane, Diana, *The Transformation of the Avant-Garde* (Chicago: University of Chicago Press, 1987).

Crossley, Ceri, and Ian Small (eds.), *Studies in Anglo-French Cultural Relations* (London: Macmillan, 1988).

Crossley, Ceri, and Ian Small (eds.), *The French Revolution and British Culture* (Oxford: Oxford University Press, 1989).

Cunningham, Gilbert F., *The Divine Comedy in English: A Critical Bibliography 1782–1900* (London: Oliver and Boyd, 1965).

Daedalus, 92 (Fall, 1963).

d'Hangest, Germain, 'Walter Pater: L'homme et L'oeuvre (Paris: Didier, 1961).

Dale, Peter Allen, '*Paracelsus* and *Sordello*: Trying the stuff of language', *Victorian Poetry*, 18 (1980), 359–69.

Dellamore, Richard, *Masculine Desire* (Chapel Hill and London: University of North Carolina Press, 1990).

Dellheim, Charles, *The Face of the Past: The preservation of the medieval inheritance in Victorian England* (Cambridge: Cambridge University Press, 1982).

de Tocqueville, Alexis, *L'Ancien Regime et la Révolution* (Paris, 1856).

Dollimore, Jonathan, 'Different desires: subjectivity and transgression in Wilde and Gide', *Textual Practice*, 1 (1987), 48–67.

Dowling, Linda, *Language and Decadence in Victorian Fin-de-Siècle* (Princeton, N.J.: Princeton University Press, 1986).

Dunn, John, 'The identity of the history of ideas', *Philosophy*, 43 (1968), 85–104.

Egbert, Donald Drew, 'The idea of the "avant-garde" in art and politics', *American Historical Review*, 73 (1967), 339–66.

Egbert, Donald Drew, *Social Radicalism and the Arts: Western Europe* (London: Duckworth, 1970).

Ekelund Jr, Robert B., and Robert F. Hébert, *A History of Economic Thinking* (London: McGraw Hill, 1975).

Ellis, Steve, *Dante and English Poetry* (Cambridge: Cambridge University Press, 1983).

Ellmann, Richard, Oscar Wilde (London: Penguin, 1988).

Faulkner, Peter (ed.), *William Morris: The critical heritage* (London: Routledge and Kegan Paul, 1973).

Faulkner, Peter, *Against the Age* (London: Allen and Unwin, 1980).

Fehér, Ferenc and Agnes Heller (eds.), *Reconstructing Aesthetics* (Oxford: Basil Blackwell, 1986).

Fennell, Francis L., *Dante Gabriel Rossetti: An annotated bibliography* (London: Garland, 1982).

Fennel, Francis L., *Dante Gabriel Rossetti: An annotated bibliography* (London: Garland, 1982).

Fischer, Walter, 'The "Poisonous Book" in Oscar Wilde's *Dorian Gray*', *Englische Studien*, 51 (1912), 37–47.

Fisher, Robert M., *The Logic of Economic Discovery: Neoclassical economics and the marginalist revolution* (Brighton: Wheatsheaf, 1986).

Fletcher, Ian and John Stokes, 'Oscar Wilde' in Richard Finneran (ed.), *Anglo-Irish Literature: A review of research* (New York: Modern Language Association of America, 1976).

Frye, Northrop, *The Great Code* (London: Routledge and Kegan Paul, 1982).

Gagnier, Regenia, '*De Profundis* as Epistola: *In Carcere et Vinculis*: a materialist reading of Oscar Wilde's autobiography', *Criticism*, 26 (1984), 335–54.

Gagnier, Regenia, *Idylls of the Market Place: Oscar Wilde and the Victorian public* (Aldershot: Scolar, 1987).

Gasset, José Ortega y, *The Dehumanization of Art and Notes on the Novel* (Princetown, N.J.: Princeton University Press, 1948).

Gauss, Charles Edward, *The Aesthetic Theories of French Artists 1855 to the present* (Baltimore: Johns Hopkins Press, 1949).

Geertz, Clifford, *The Interpretation of Cultures* (New York: Basic Books, 1973).

Giddens, Anthony, 'Modernism and postmodernism', *New German Critique*, 22 (Winter, 1981), 15–18.

Gilman, Richard, 'The idea of the avant-garde', *Partisan Review*, 39 (1972), 382–96.

Goldstein, Doris, 'The organizational development of the British historical profession, 1884–1921', *Bulletin of the Institute of Historical Research*, 55 (1982), 180–93.

Goldstein, Doris, 'The professionalization of history in Britain in the late nineteenth and early twentieth centuries', *Storia Della Storiografia*, 1 (1983), 3–27.

Gooch, G. P., *History and Historians in the Nineteenth Century* (2nd edn, London: Longman, 1952).

Goode, John, 'William Morris and the Dream of Revolution' in John Lucas (ed.), *Literature and Politics in the Nineteenth Century* (London: Methuen, 1971), 221–78.

Gosse, Edmund, *A Short History of English Literature* (London: Heinemann, 1898).

Greenblatt, Stephen, *Shakesperian Negotiations* (Oxford: Clarendon Press, 1988).

Grennan, Margaret, *William Morris: Medievalist and revolutionary* (New York: King's Crown Press, 1954).

Guy, Josephine, 'The concept of tradition and late nineteenth-century British avant-garde movements', *Prose Studies*, 3 (September 1990), 250–60.

Guy, Josephine and Ian Small, 'Usefulness in literary history', *British Journal of Aesthetics* (Spring, 1991).

Guy, Josephine, Ian Small and Marcus Walsh, 'The profession of English', *English Association Newsletter*, nos 131 and 132.

Habermas, Jürgen, 'Modernity versus postmodernity', *New German Critique*, 22 (Winter, 1981), 3–14.

Halsey, A. H., and Trow, M. A. *The British Academics* (London: Faber and Faber, 1971).

Hamilton, Walter, *The Aesthetic Movement in England* (London: Reeves and Turner, 1882).

Harris, Wendell, 'Arnold, Pater, Wilde, and the Object as in Themselves They See It', *Studies in English Literature*, 11 (1971), 733–47.

Harskamp, J. T., 'Contemporaneity, Modernism, Avant-Garde', *British Journal of Aesthetics*, 20 (1980), 204–14.

Harvie, Christopher, *The Lights of Liberalism* (London: Allen Lane, 1976).

Hawthorn, Geoffrey, *Enlightenment and Despair: A history of social theory* (2nd edn, Cambridge: Cambridge University Press, 1987).

Hemmings, F. W. J., *Culture and Society in France 1848–1898* (London: Batsford, 1971).

Hemmings, F. W. J., *Culture and Society in France 1789–1848* (Leicester: Leicester University Press, 1987).

Henderson, Philip, *Swinburne: The Portrait of a Poet* (London: Routledge and Kegan Paul, 1978).

Hess, Thomas B., and John Ashbery (eds.), *The Avant-Garde, Art News Annual*, 34 (1968).

Heyck, T. W., *The Transformation of Intellectual Life in Victorian England* (London: Croom Helm, 1982).

Heyck, T. W., 'The idea of a university in Britain, 1870–1970', *History of European Ideas*, 8 (1987), 205–19.

Hodgson, Amanda, *The Romances of William Morris* (Cambridge: Cambridge University Press, 1987).

Hohendahl, Peter Uwe, 'The loss of reality: Gottfried Benn's early prose' in Andreas Huyssen and David Bathrick, (eds.), *Modernity and the Text* (New York: Columbia University Press, 1989), 81–94.

Hospers, John (ed.), *Introductory Readings in Aesthetics* (London: The Free Press, 1969).

Humble, P. N., 'The philosophic challenge of the avant-garde', *British Journal of Aesthetics*, 24 (1984), 119–28.

Hunt, William Holman, *Pre-Raphaelitism and the Pre-Raphaelite Brotherhood* (London: Macmillan, 1905).

Hutchison, T. W., *A Review of Economic Doctrines 1870–1929* (Westport, Conn.: The Greenwood Press, 1975).

Hutchison, T. W., *On Revolutions and Progress in Economic Knowledge* (Cambridge: Cambridge University Press, 1978).

Huyssen, Andreas, 'The search for tradition: avant-garde and postmodernism in the 1970s', *New German Critique*, 22 (Winter, 1981), 23–40.

Huyssen, Andreas, *After The Great Divide: Modernism, mass culture and postmodernism* (London: Macmillan, 1988).

Huyssen, Andreas and David Bathrick (eds.), *Modernity and the Text* (New York: Columbia University Press, 1989).

Hyder, Clyde K. (ed.), *Swinburne: The critical heritage* (London: Routledge and Kegan Paul, 1970).

Hyder, Clyde K. (ed.), *Swinburne as Critic* (London: Routledge and Kegan Paul, 1972).

Jackson, J. A., (ed.), *Professions and Professionalization* (London: Cambridge University Press, 1970).

Jackson, Russell (ed.), *Oscar Wilde: The Importance of Being Earnest* (London: Ernest Benn, 1980).

Russell Jackson, 'A classic without danger: The National Theatre's *The Importance of Being Earnest*', *Critical Quarterly*, 25 (1983), 73–80.

Jackson, Russell, *Victorian Theatre* (London: A. and C. Black, 1989).

Jackson, Russell, and Ian Small (eds.), *Oscar Wilde: Two Society Comedies* (London: Ernest Benn, 1980).

Jann, Rosemary, 'From amateur to professional: The case of the Oxbridge historians', *Journal of British Studies*, 2 (1983), 122–47.

Johnson, Lionel, 'For a Little Clan', *Academy* (13 October 1890).

Johnson, Pauline, *Marxist Aesthetics* (London: Routledge and Kegan Paul, 1984).

Johnson, R. V., *Aestheticism* (London: Methuen, 1969)

Jones, Peter, *'The Theory of the Avant-Garde.* By Renato Poggioli', *British Journal of Aesthetics*, 9 (1969), 84–9.

Jowett, Benjamin, *The Republic of Plato* (Oxford: Clarendon Press, 1876).

Karl, Frederick R., *Modern and Modernism* (New York: Atheneum, 1985).

Kearney, Anthony, *John Churton Collins: The louse on the locks of literature* (Edinburgh: Scottish Academic Press, 1986).

Kent, Christopher, *Brains and Numbers: Elitism, Comtism and democracy in mid-Victorian Britain* (London: University of Toronto Press, 1978).

Khattab, Ezzat Abdulmajeed, 'The critical reception of Browning's The Ring and the Book: 1868–1889 and 1951–1968', *Salzburg Studies in English Literature*, 66 (1977), 1–214.

Kingsley, Charles, *The Limits of Exact Science as Applied to History* (Cambridge: J. H. Parker and Son, 1860).

Koot, Gerald M., 'English historical economics and the emergence of economic history in England', *History of Political Economy*, 12 (1980), 174–205.

Kramer, Hilton, *The Age of the Avant-Garde* (London: Secker and Warburg, 1974).

Rosalind Krauss, *The Originality of the Avant-Garde and Other Modernist Myths* (Cambridge, Mass.: MIT Press, 1985).

Landow, George P., *The Aesthetic and Critical Theories of John Ruskin* (Princeton, N.J.: Princeton University Press, 1971).

Landow, George P., *William Holman Hunt and Typological Symbolism* (London: Yale University Press, 1979).

Larson, M. S., *The Rise of Professionalism: a sociological analysis* (London: University of California Press, 1977).

Levine, Phillipa, *The Amateur and the Professional: Antiquarians, historians and archaeologists in Victorian England, 1838–1886* (Cambridge: Cambridge University Press, 1986).

Litzinger, Boyd, and Donald Smalley (eds.), *Robert Browning: The critical heritage* (London: Routledge and Kegan Paul, 1970).

Lukács, Georg, *The Meaning of Contemporary Realism* (London: Merlin Press, 1972).

Macaulay, Thomas Babington, 'Hallam's constitutional history', *Edinburgh Review*, 48 (1828), 96–169.

Macaulay, Thomas Babington, 'Dumont's *Recollections of Mirabeau* – The French Revolution', *Edinburgh Review*, 55 (1832), 552–76.

Macaulay, Thomas Babington, *Critical and Historical Essays*, 3 vols. (London: Longman, 1843).

Macaulay, Thomas Babington, *The History of England*, 5 vols. (London: Longman, 1849–61).

Macaulay, Thomas Babington, *Napoleon and the Restoration of the Bourbons*, ed. Joseph Hamburger (London: Longman, 1977).

Mackintosh, Sir James, *History of the Revolution in England in 1688* (London: Longman, 1834).

Maloney, John, *Marshall, Orthodoxy and the Professionalization of Economics* (Cambridge: Cambridge University Press, 1985).

The Manchester School, 2 (May, 1951).

Mandelbaum, Maurice, *History, Man and Reason: A study in nineteenth century thought* (London: Johns Hopkins Press, 1971).

Mansel, Henry, *Prolegomena Logica* (Oxford: William Graham, 1851).

Mansel, Henry, *The Philosophy of the Conditioned* (London: Alexander Strahan, 1866).

Margolis, Joseph (ed.), *Philosophy Looks at the Arts* (New York: Charles Scribner and Sons, 1962).

Marshall, Alfred, 'Distribution and exchange', *Economic Journal*, 8 (1898), 37–59.

Maurer, Oscar, 'A philistine source for *Dorian Gray*', *Philological Quarterly*, 26 (1947), 84–6.

Meier, Paul, *William Morris: The Marxist Dreamer*, 2 vols. (Brighton: Harvester, 1978).

Mellon, Stanley, *The Political uses of History: A study of historians in the Restoration* (Stanford: Stanford University Press, 1958).

Michelet, Jules, *Histoire de la Révolution Française*, Revised edn, Paris, 1869).

François, Mignet, *Histoire de La Révolution Française* (16th edn, Paris, 1887).

Mill, John Stuart, *A System of Logic: Ratiocinative and inductive*, 2 vols. (London: John W. Parker, 1848).

Mill, John Stuart, 'Thoughts on poetry and its varieties', *Collected Works of John Stuart Mill*, I, eds. John M. Robson and Jack Stillinger (London: University of Toronto Press, 1981a), 341–66.

Mill, John Stuart, *Autobiography, Collected Works of John Stuart Mill*, I, eds. John M. Robson and Jack Stillinger (London: University of Toronto Press, 1981b), 1–290.

Millerson, Geoffrey, *The Qualifying Associations: A study in professionalization* (London: Routledge and Kegan Paul, 1964).

Milne, A. T., 'History at the universities: then and now', *History*, 59 (1974), 33–46.

Monsman, Gerald, 'Pater's Aesthetic Hero', *University of Toronto Quarterly*, 40 (1971), 136–51.

Morley, John, *On the Study of Literature* (Edinburgh: R. and C. Clark, 1887).

Morris, May, (ed.), *William Morris: Artist, Writer, Socialist*, 2 vols. (Oxford: Basil Blackwell, 1936).

Morris, William, *The Collected Works of William Morris*, ed. May Morris, (London: Longman, 1910–15).

Moulton, Richard G., *The Reorganisation of Liberal Education* (Cambridge: Leader and Sons, 1880).

Murray, Isobel, 'The strange case of Dr Jekyll and Oscar Wilde', *Durham University Journal*, 79 (1987a), 311–19.

Murray, Isobel, '*Children of Tomorrow*: a Sharp inspiration for *Dorian Gray*', *Durham University Journal*, 80 (1987b), 69–76.

Myers, F. W., 'Rossetti and the religion of beauty', *The Cornhill Magazine*, 47 (1883), 213–24.

Nisbett, R. A., 'Conservatism and Sociology', *American Journal of Sociology*, LVIII (1952), 167–75.

Nochlin, Linda, 'The invention of the avant-garde in France, 1830–80', in Thomas B. Hess and John Ashbery (eds.), *The Avant-Garde, Art News Annual*, 34 (1968), 16.

Nochlin, Linda, *Realism* (London: Penguin, 1971).

Nochlin, Linda, *Gustave Courbet: A study of style and society* (New York: Garland, 1976).

Osborne, Harold (ed.), *Aesthetics* (Oxford: Oxford University Press, 1972).

Owen, John E., *L. T. Hobhouse, Sociologist* (London: Thames Nelson and Sons, 1974).

Pater, Walter, *Plato and Platonism* (London: Macmillan, 1893).

Pater, Walter, 'Dante Gabriel Rossetti' in Thomas Humphrey Ward (ed.), *The English Poets*, 4 (London: Macmillan, 1894), 633–41.

Pater, Walter, 'Shadwell's Dante', *Uncollected Essays by Walter Pater* (Portland, Maine: Thomas B. Mosher, 1903), 145–61.

Pater, Walter, 'A review of Arthur Symons's *An Introduction to the Study of Browning*, in Walter Pater, *Essays from 'The Guardian'* (London: Macmillan 1906), 41–51.

Pater, Walter, *Appreciations* (London: Macmillan, 1913).

Pater, Walter, *The Renaissance*, ed. Donald Hill (Berkeley, Ca.: University of California Press, 1980).

Pater, Walter, *Marius the Epicurean*, ed. Ian Small (Oxford: Oxford University Press, 1986).

Patten, Robert L., ' "The people have set literature free": The professionalization of letters in nineteenth-century England', *Review*, 9 (1987), 1–34.

Pattison, Mrs Mark, 'Art', *Westminster Review*, 43 (1873), 638–45.

Peckham, Morse, 'Thoughts on editing *Sordello*', *Studies in Browning and his Circle*, 5 (1977), 11–18.

Peterson, William S., *Interrogating the Oracle: A history of the London Browning Society* (Athens, Ohio: Ohio University Press, 1969).

Peyre, Henri, 'Three nineteenth century myths: race, nation, revolution' in Henri Peyre, *Historical and Critical Essays* (Nebraska: University of Nebraska Press, 1968), 24–61.

Pick, John, 'Divergent disciples of Walter Pater', *Thought*, 23 (1948), 114–28.

Poggioli, Renato, *The Theory of the Avant-Garde* (Cambridge, Mass.: Harvard University Press, 1968).

Powell, Kerry, 'Hawthorne, Arlo Bates and *The Picture of Dorian Gray*', *Papers in Language and Literature*, 16 (1980), 403–16.

Powell, Kerry, 'Tom, Dick and Dorian Gray: magic-picture mania in late Victorian fiction', *Philological Quarterly*, 62 (1983), 147–70.

Powell, Kerry, 'The mesmerizing of Dorian Gray', *Victorian Newsletter*, 65 (1984), 20.

Powell, Kerry, 'Wilde and Ibsen', *English Literature in Transition*, 28 (1985), 224–42.

Raby, Peter, *Oscar Wilde* (Cambridge: Cambridge University Press, 1988).

Reader, W. J., *Professional Men: The rise of the professional classes in nineteenth-century Britain* (London: Weidenfeld and Nicolson, 1966).

Reff, Theodore, *Manet: Olympia* (London: Allen Lane, 1976).

Roberts, J. M., *The French Revolution* (Oxford: Oxford University Press, 1978).

Robertson, John Mackinnon, *Buckle and his Critics: A study in sociology* (London: Swan Sonnenschein and Co., 1895).

Robinson, James K., 'A Neglected Phase of the aesthetic movement: English parnassianism', *PMLA*, 68 (1953), 175–54.

Robson, John M. and Jack Stillinger (eds.), *Autobiography, Collected works of John Stuart Mill*, I (London: University of Toronto Press, 1981).

Rorty, Richard, J. B. Schneewind and Quentin Skinner (eds.), *Philosophy in History: Essays on the historiography of philosophy* (Cambridge: Cambridge University Press, 1984).

Charles Rosen, *Schoenberg* (London: Marion Boyars, 1976).

Charles Rosen and Henri Zerner, *Romanticism and Realism: The mythology of nineteenth-century art* (London: Faber and Faber, 1984).

Rosenberg, Harold, 'Collective, ideological, combative', in Thomas B. Hess and John Ashbery (eds.), *The Avant-Garde, Art News Annual*, 34 (1968), 75.

Rossetti, Dante Gabriel, '*Madeline* with other poems and parables by Thomas Gordon Hake, M.D.', *The Academy* (1 February 1871), 105–7.

Rossetti, Dante Gabriel, *Poems* (London: Ellis, 1881a).

Rossetti, Dante Gabriel, *Ballads and Sonnets* (London: Ellis, 1881b).

Rothblatt, Sheldon, *The Revolution of the Dons* (London: Faber and Faber, 1968).

Rothblatt, Sheldon, *Tradition and Change in English Liberal Education* (London: Faber, 1976).

St Aubyn, Giles, *A Victorian Eminence* (London: Barrie Books, 1958).

Sambrook, James (ed.), *Pre-Raphaelitism* (London: University of Chicago Press, 1974).

Samuels, Warren, 'The history of economic thought as intellectual history', *History of Political Economy*, 6 (1974), 305–25.

Schapiro, Meyer, 'Courbet and popular imagery: An essay on Realism and Naïveté', *Journal of the Warburg and Courtauld Institute*, 4 (1940–1), 164–91.

Schulte-Sasse, Jochan, 'Foreword: theory of modernism versus theory of the avant-garde', in Bürger, *Theory of the Avant-Garde* (Manchester: Manchester University Press, 1984), vii–xlvii.

Scruton, Roger, 'Man's second disobedience: a vindication of Burke', in Ceri Crossley and Ian Small (eds.), *The French Revolution and British Culture* (Oxford: Oxford University Press, 1989), 187–222.

Seiler, R. M. (ed.), *Walter Pater: The critical heritage* (London: Routledge and Kegan Paul, 1980).

Shairp, John Campbell, 'Aesthetic poetry: Dante Gabriel Rossetti', *Contemporary Review*, 42 (1882a), 17–32.

Shairp, John Campbell, 'English poets and Oxford critics', *Quarterly Review*, 153 (1882b), 413–63.

Shannon, Richard, *The Crisis of Imperialism 1865–1915* (London: Hart-Davis Macgibbon, 1974).

Shapiro, Theda, *Painters and Politics: The European avant-garde and society, 1900–1925* (Amsterdam: Elsevier, 1976).

Shuter, William F., 'Pater's Reshuffled Text', *Nineteenth Century Literature*, 31 (1989), 500–25.

Siegal, Sandra, 'Wilde's use and abuse of aphorism', *Victorian Studies, Association of Western Canada Newsletter*, 12 (1986), 16–26.

Skinner, Quentin, 'Meaning and understanding in the history of ideas', *History and Theory*, 8 (1969), 3–53.

Sloane, Joseph, *French Painting between the Past and the Present* (Princeton, N.J.: Princeton University Press, 1951).

Small, Ian, 'Plato and Pater: Fin-de-Siècle Aesthetics', *British Journal of Aesthetics*, 12 (1972), 369–83.

Small, Ian, *The Aesthetes* (London: Routledge and Kegan Paul, 1979).

Small, Ian, *Conditions for Criticism: Authority, knowledge and literature in the late nineteenth century* (Oxford: Clarendon Press, 1991).

Small, Ian and Josephine Guy, 'Critical opinion: English in crisis', *Essays in Criticism*, 39 (July 1989), 185–95.

Small, Ian and Josephine Guy, 'English in crisis – II', *Essays in Criticism*, 40 (July 1990), 105–197.

Small, Ian and Russell Jackson (eds.), 'Introduction', *Oscar Wilde, Two Society Comedies* (London: Ernest Benn, 1983).

Smith, Goldwin, *Lectures on Modern History Delivered at Oxford 1859–61* (Oxford: J. H. Parker and Son, 1861).

Spencer, Herbert, *Essays: Scientific, Political, Theological* (London: Williams and Norgate, 1868).

Spencer, Herbert, *The Study of Sociology* (London: Kegan, Paul and Trench, 1873).

Spencer, Herbert, *Principles of Sociology*, 3 vols. (London: Williams and Norgate, 1876–96).

Spencer, Herbert, *The Study of Sociology* (13th edn., London: Henry S. King, 1887).

Spivey, Ted, 'Damnation and salvation in *The Picture of Dorian Gray*', *Boston University Studies in English*, 4 (1960), 162–70.

Stanford, Derek, (ed.), *Pre-Raphaelite Writing* (London: Dent, 1973).

Statham, Henry, 'Rossetti's Poems', *Edinburgh Review*, 155 (1882), 322–37.

Stubbs, William, *Seventeen Lectures on the Study of Medieval and Modern History and Kindred Subjects* (3rd edn., Oxford: Clarendon Press, 1900).

Sussman, Herbert L., *Fact into Figure: Typology in Carlyle, Ruskin and the Pre-Raphaelite Brotherhood* (Columbus, Ohio: Ohio University Press, 1979).

Swinburne, Algernon Charles, 'The poems of Dante Gabriel Rossetti', *Fortnightly Review*, 7 n.s. (1870), 551–79.

Swinburne, Algernon Charles, *George Chapman* (London: Macmillan, 1875).

Szacki, Jerzy, *History of Sociological Thought* (London: Aldwych Press, 1979).

Taylor, Ronald (ed. and trans.), *Aesthetics and Politics* (London: Verso, 1977).

Temple, Ruth Z., 'Truth in labelling: Pre-Raphaelitism, Aestheticism, Decadence, Fin de Siècle', *English Literature in Transition*, 17 (1970), 201–22.

Thomas, Donald, *Swinburne: The poet and his world* (London: Weidenfeld and Nicolson, 1979).

Thompson, E. P., *William Morris: Romantic to revolutionary* (London: Lawrence Wishart, 1955).

Thornton, R. K. R., *The Decadent Dilemma* (London: Edward Arnold, 1983).

Tilley, Arthur, 'Two theories of poetry', *Macmillan's Magazine*, 44 (1881), 268–79.

Tressell, Robert, *The Ragged Trousered Philanthropists* (London: Grant Richards, 1914).

Trevelyan, Lady (ed.), *The Works of Lord Macaulay* (London: Longman, 1897).

Tucker, Paul, 'Browning, Pater and the Hellenic ideal', *Browning Society Notes*, 19 (1979), 2–7.

Turner, Jonathan H., *Herbert Spencer: A renewed appreciation* (London: Sage, 1985).

Unsigned review, 'Art 5: The poetry of Rossetti', *British Quarterly*, 76 (1882), 109–27.

Ward, Thomas Humphrey (ed.), *The English Poets*, vol. 4 (London: Macmillan, 1894).

Watson, Edward A., 'Wilde's iconoclastic classicism: "The Critic as Artist"', *English Literature in Transition*, 27 (1984), 225–35.

Wees, William C., *Vorticism and the English Avant-Garde* (Manchester: Manchester University Press, 1972).

Weightman, John, *The Concept of the Avant-Garde* (London: Alcove Press, 1973).

Weisberg, Gabriel P., *The Realist Tradition: French painting and drawing 1830–1900* (Cleveland, Ohio: Cleveland Museum of Art, 1980).

Weisberg, Gabriel P. (ed.), *The European Realist Tradition* (Bloomington, Indiana: Indiana University Press, 1982).

White, Allon, *The Uses of Obscurity* (London: Routledge and Kegan Paul, 1981).

Whitla, William, 'Browning, Alfred Austin and the Byron Scandal', *Browning Society Notes*, 7 (1977), 12–32.

Wilde, Oscar, *Complete Works*, (ed.) Robert Ross (London: Methuen and Co., 1912).

Wilde, Oscar, *Essays and Lectures* (London: Methuen, 1913).

Wilde, Oscar, *The Works of Oscar Wilde*, ed. G. F. Maine (London: Collins, 1949).

Williams, Carolyn, 'Typology as narrative form: The temporal logic of *Marius*', *English Literature in Transition*, 27 (1984), 11–13.

Williams, Raymond, *Culture and Society* (Harmondsworth: Chatto and Windus, 1968).

Wolff, Janet, *The Social Production of Art* (London: Macmillan, 1981).

Wollheim, Richard, 'Sociological explanation of the arts' in Milton C. Albrecht and James H. Barnett (eds.), *The Sociology of Art and Literature: A reader* (London: Duckworth, 1970), 574–81.

Wollheim, Richard, *Art and its Objects* (2nd edn., Cambridge: Cambridge University Press, 1980).

Woodcock, George, *Anarchism* (Harmonsworth: Penguin, 1963).

Woodcock, George, *The Paradox of Oscar Wilde* (London: T. V. Boardman, 1949).

Woodcock, George, 'The meaning of revolution in Britain: 1770–1800', in Ceri Crossley and Ian Small (eds.), *The French Revolution and British Culture* (Oxford: Oxford University Press, 1989), 1–30.

Woodward, Llewllyn, 'The rise of the professonial historian' in K. Bourne and D. C. Watt (eds.), *Studies in International History* (London: Longman, 1987), 16–34.

Worth, Katherine, *Oscar Wilde* (London: Macmillan, 1983).

Wright, T. R., *The Religion of Humanity* (Cambridge: Cambridge University Press, 1986).

Index